Evil
and the
Christian
God

Michael Peterson

BAKER BOOK HOUSE
Grand Rapids, Michigan 49506

For
Rebecca

Contents

Preface

Perhaps the most important and most enduring challenge to Christian belief is the problem of evil. For many thoughtful persons, evil in the world seems incongruous with Christian claims about the perfect goodness and absolute power of God. Other conceptions of God, of course, generate their own peculiar problems of evil, but the Christian conception raises the difficulty to greatest proportions. Christian theists claim so much for the nature and purposes of God that they have much to explain. As a Christian theist, my purpose in this book is to provide a response to the problem of evil. The response is primarily intended to remove the apparent incompatibility between God and evil, and thus avoid the atheistic conclusion which critics frequently reach. A secondary thesis is that the character of evil in the world actually supports a theistic conception of reality.

The book takes seriously the concerns and arguments of thinkers who are not Christian theists, and hence may be sympathetically read by those who are not already convinced that theism is true. The study is based on a vast amount of technical literature on the problem of evil, but does not assume any sort of philosophical specialization on the part of the reader. This is not to deny, however, that some points can be given technical expression and defense. Therefore, the present treatment offers something both for the student and for the scholar.

The structure of the book is very simple. Chapter 1 records the disturbing presence of evil in human life and shows that it seems to damage the credibility of Christian theology. The next two chapters examine two different ways in which the problem of evil has been posed as a theoretical difficulty. Chapter 2 focuses on the logical version of the problem of evil and chapter 3 on the evidential version of the problem. After evaluating the relative strengths of these versions of the problem of evil, it is found that one particular formulation of the evidential version is most formidable: the argument from apparently gratuitous evil. The argument from gratuitous evil occupies the rest of the book. In chapter 4 this argument is analyzed and alternatives for reply are assessed. Chapter 5 contains a reply tracing the implications which the concepts of free will, natural law, and soul-making have for the issue of gratuitous evil in a theistic order. In chapter 6, what might be called the existential dimension of the problem of gratuitous evil is examined in light of the theoretical dimension.

A project such as this one is seldom a purely private undertaking. Three institutions have provided valuable assistance. I am grateful to the Institute for Advanced Christian Studies for timely grants which covered my research and writing during 1979 and 1980. I am also indebted to the National Endowment for the Humanities for the opportunity to do preliminary outlining at a 1978 summer seminar. Also, in 1978, the Faculty Research and Development Committee of Asbury College provided a grant for materials.

A number of individuals have greatly contributed to various phases of this project. I owe to Edward Madden, teacher and friend, the original inspiration for the book. His work on evil, frequently done in conjunction with Peter Hare, made me feel the force of the problem of gratuitous evil and the need for a response. I am indebted to Alvin Plantinga, Bruce Reichenbach, David Basinger, William Hasker, Paul Vincent, and James Hamilton for helpful comments on many ideas and arguments which are incorporated into the book. Mary Olson, Beverly Fischer, Sherry Plyman, Teri Conwell, Rose Heitkamp, and Nancy Baker conscientiously typed portions of the manuscript. Tim Lang diligently helped proofread the final draft.

Still, there is another whose influence on this book is more pervasive and profound than that of any other. My wife, Rebecca, made necessary sacrifices and gave sustaining encouragement throughout its preparation. So, as with any good thing that I have ever done, this piece is as much hers as it is mine. With both humility and pride I dedicate it to her.

Michael L. Peterson
Department of Philosophy
Asbury College

1

Evil and Christianity

Evil in Human Existence

The radical and pervasive presence of evil cannot be ignored or explained away. Whether evil occurs in natural catastrophes, such as epidemics and earthquakes, or in manmade horrors, such as the Holocaust and Jonestown, it meets us at every turn and forces each of us to ponder the meaning of existence. It is not surprising that, more than any other theme, the perennial problem of evil haunts those areas of inquiry which deal primarily with the nature and destiny of man: philosophy, theology, literature, art, and history. Neither is it surprising that every major world-view, whether religious, ethical, or political, proposes some insight into this vexing problem.

One of the deepest human impulses is the resistance to evil. Laymen and scholars attempt to explain, in their own ways, the phenomenon of evil. In practical life, the resistance to evil surfaces in efforts to minimize and combat the negative aspects of existence. However, the feebleness and failure of efforts to shut evil out, to master it, to understand it, simply exacerbate the problem. The problem is indeed an inveterate one and is no less serious today than it was centuries ago.

Over two thousand years ago, the subject of evil came

under discussion in Aristotle's *Poetics*. Aristotle recognized that tragic drama presents a hero whose highest virtues somehow precipitate fault. The tragic hero represents the universal experience of mankind, and by emotional identification with his *hamartia* (sin, flaw), the audience undergoes catharsis (purging of the emotions).[1] Of course, the universal experience of mankind in dealing with evils of its own creation is not simply an emotional matter. The mind confronts the evils which threaten to destroy the fragile and fleeting goods of human life and searches for an answer. Perhaps an appropriate catharsis for the mind is harder for our generation to find than anything else.

Human moral evil is not the only force which tends to thwart all that we hold dear. The best of us are sometimes hurt and even crushed by the impersonal forces of the universe. These forces know nothing of human agendas or purposes, and also call into question the significance of personal existence. Herman Melville captured this in *Moby Dick*. Captain Ahab of the *Pequod*, forty years a whaler in the first half of the last century, set out from Nantucket on what appeared to be a long whaling cruise. Little did anyone know that Ahab's journey was not seaman's business, but a quest for the meaning of life.

Ahab had lost a leg in an earlier encounter with Moby Dick, a great white whale, then the terror of the seas, and was now bent on destroying it. The captain was obsessed with the meaning of human existence in the face of overwhelming natural forces. Ironically, the whale was white, a color which normally symbolizes what is thought to be sacred and holy; but the whale was fearsome and hostile to human values, and in the end, triumphant. Ishmael, the only survivor, claims that in losing his life Ahab dis-

---

1. In addition to Aristotle's *Poetics*, see Henry Myers, *Tragedy: A View of Life* (Ithaca, NY: Cornell University, 1956), pp. 28–53.

covered its meaning.[2] The modern world knows all too well that this disturbing picture of life—its being ruined and finally snuffed out by forces beyond its control—is a realistic one.

There are those who do not share the view that there is a capacity for evil in both man and nature. From the romantic optimism of Jean Jacques Rousseau to the technological optimism of Buckminster Fuller, some have sought to build a world in which sorrow and struggle are no longer the price of true happiness. The historian H. G. Wells expressed this position in *A Short History of the World:*

> Can we doubt that presently our race will more than re-alize our boldest imaginations, that it will achieve unity and peace, that it will live, the children of our blood will live, in a world made more splendid and lovely than any palace or garden that we know, going on from strength to strength in an ever-widening circle of adventure and achievement? What man has done, the little triumphs of his present state. . . form the prelude to the things that man has yet to do.[3]

But the outbreak of World War II shattered Wells's fond dreams and elicited an increasingly pessimistic view of man's existence:

> In spite of all my disposition to a brave-looking optimism, I perceive that now the universe is bored with [man], is turning a hard face to him, and I see him being carried . . . along the stream of fate to degradation, suffering and death.[4]

2. In addition to *Moby Dick*, see Myers, *Tragedy*, pp. 57–77, and Richard Sewall, *The Vision of Tragedy* (New Haven, CT: Yale University, 1959), pp. 92–105.

3. H. G. Wells, *A Short History of the World* (Harmondsworth: Pelican, 1937), p. 289.

4. H. G. Wells, *The Fate of Homo Sapiens* (London: Secker and Warburg, 1939), p. 312.

Whether the universe or fate or man himself is blamed, when unbridled optimism gains ascendancy, it sooner or later becomes indefensible and is abandoned. The problem of evil refuses to be dismissed.

One does not have to consult the experience of mankind through the ages to recognize the depth and scope of the problem of evil. In this day of newspapers, radio, and television, every sensitive person is vividly aware of the pain and anguish of others. Images of starving children in Kampuchea, the brutal Soviet invasion of Afghanistan, political executions in Iran, a destructive earthquake in Italy, and countless other scenes impress upon our consciousness the disturbing presence of evil.

As contemporary persons ponder the bearing of evil on the meaning of human life, they are often tempted to conclude with Ecclesiastes: "Vanity of vanities! All is vanity" (1:2). The chorus in T. S. Eliot's *Murder in the Cathedral* echoes this pessimistic complaint:

> Here is no continuing city, here
> is no abiding stay.
> Ill the wind, ill the time, uncertain
> the profit, certain the danger.
>
> O late late late, late is the time,
> too late, and rotten the year;
> Evil the wind, and bitter the sea, and
> grey the sky, grey grey grey.[5]

This unfortunate interpretation of life appears to be natural and warranted when the facts of evil are taken seriously.

In *The Sacred Canopy* Peter Berger writes that every religion imposes order and lawfulness on events and ex-

5. T. S. Eliot, *Murder in the Cathedral: The Complete Poems* (New York: Harcourt, Brace and Co., 1952), p. 180.

periences which seem to be chaotic and destructive—most notably, the phenomena of suffering, evil, and death. According to Berger, religion, as a social enterprise, donates to the individual a *nomos*, or lawful explanation, for understanding the otherwise anomic features of his existence.[6] In traditional terminology, religion provides a *theodicy*, or a "justification of the ways of God to man" (after John Milton). In the words of Berger's title, religion brings life under a "sacred canopy" by positing a higher meaning and authority. Berger is worth quoting at length on this point:

> The anomic phenomena must not only be lived through, they must also be explained—to wit, explained in terms of the nomos established in the society in question. An explanation of these phenomena in terms of religious legitimations, of whatever degree of theoretical sophistication, may be called a theodicy. It is important to stress here particularly (although the same point has already been made generally with respect to religious legitimations) that such an explanation need not entail a complex theoretical system. The illiterate peasant who comments upon the death of a child by referring to the will of God is engaging in theodicy as much as the learned theologian who writes a treatise to demonstrate that the suffering of the innocent does not negate the conception of a God both all-good and all-powerful. All the same, it is possible to differentiate theodicies in terms of their degree of rationality, that is, the degree to which they entail a theory that coherently and consistently explains the phenomena in question in terms of an over-all view of the universe. Such a theory, of course, once it is socially established, may be refracted on different levels of sophistication throughout the society. Thus, the peasant, when he speaks about the

6. Peter Berger, *The Sacred Canopy* (New York: Doubleday, 1967), especially chapters 1–3.

will of God, may himself intend, however inarticulately, the majestic theodicy constructed by the theologian.[7]

So, what a religious system says about evil reveals a great deal about what it takes ultimate reality, and man's relation to it, to be. Hence, the credibility of a religion is closely linked to its ability to explain evil.

The Challenge to Christianity

The problem of evil is most acute for orthodox Christian theology because two of its important beliefs seem to be incompatible. On the one hand, Christian theology affirms the unrivaled power, unlimited knowledge, and unrelenting love of God. On the other hand, Christian theology recognizes the obvious fact that horrendous evils occur in God's created order. To many persons it seems that the Christian God—if He really exists and is the source and guarantor of value—would not allow the world to be as it is. This is the crux of the problem for Christian belief. Down through history, Christian theologians and philosophers have wrestled with this problem. Thoughtful and sensitive laity have also felt the need for at least a general explanation of evil.

It is obvious that the problem of evil is a major obstacle for Christian apologetics in our time. Some thinkers believe that unless Christians have a rational solution to the problem of evil they have no right to hold their distinctive theological position or to ask others to adopt it.[8] Philos-

7. Ibid., pp. 53–54.
8. In response, some Christians hold that believers may instead produce an argument to the effect that they do not need a theodicy. A number of approaches are possible here. For example, a believer may argue that since the problem of evil does not conclusively disprove his position, he need not answer it. Or a believer may argue that he has convincing proof of God's

opher T. W. Settle argues that grappling with the problem of evil is a "prolegomenon to intellectually honest theology."[9] Thor Hall proposes that the ability or inability to generate an answer to the vexing problem of evil is the index of the "reasonableness of theology." Hall says that Christian thinkers must "be capable of handling honestly the actualities of human existence (realities which we all know) while at the same time providing a framework for explicating responsibly the essential affirmations of the faith (affirmations which are given within the historical tradition)."[10] Sensing the prominence of evil, and particularly the evil of suffering, in the modern mind's quest for meaning, Arthur McGill contends that "no theological investigation can be genuinely Christian which is not genuinely open to the unbeliever and which does not include the unbeliever in its probing efforts."[11] Consequently, the nature of our response to the problem of suffering is a basic "test of theological method."

The purpose of this book is to arrive at a response to the problem of evil as it arises for orthodox Christian theology. Essentially, our response will support what is generally referred to here as Christian theism or just theism—the position that God exists and is omnipotent, omniscient, and wholly good. And further, our response will support Christian theism, not only by defending it from

---

existence on other grounds, and hence that he knows that the problem of evil must have some answer. Presently, there do not appear to be any such arguments which can be comfortably accepted. Christian theism purports to explain relevant features of human existence, but evil does not appear to fit well into that explanation. Therefore, there is at least a *prima facie* case that the Christian theist must make good his claim by handling the problem of evil.

9. T. W. Settle, "A Prolegomenon to Intellectually Honest Theology," *The Philosophical Forum* 1 (1978): 136–40.

10. Thor Hall, "Theodicy as Test of the Reasonableness of Theology," *Religion in Life* 43 (1974): 204.

11. Arthur McGill, *Suffering: A Test of Theological Method* (Philadelphia: Geneva, 1968), p. 24.

the attack based on the presence of evil, but also by showing that it explains the character of evil in a conceptually adequate way.

Our concern with the theistic basis of Christianity may seem puzzling. Some critics, for example, note that the term *theism* involves applying to God impersonal, static concepts from classical Greek metaphysics (e.g., omnipotence and omniscience), as opposed to the personal, dynamic concepts of the biblical tradition (e.g., love and mercy). Hence, a defense of theism against the problem of evil, or any other rational objection for that matter, has little to do with maintaining true Christianity. However, this kind of criticism fails to recognize that theistic concepts are essential to orthodox Christianity. The fact that similar concepts occur in non-Christian or pre-Christian thought may simply be evidence that some truths about God are available to all. Orthodox Christians must hold that God is unlimited in power, knowledge, and goodness, though their distinctive emphasis is on the work of Jesus Christ and man's relation to Him. Assertions about God's perfect attributes constitute a large part of the theoretical foundation upon which claims about Jesus Christ, as well as other orthodox claims, make sense. If the foundation is removed, then the import of Christian theology is either altered or lost. As Norman Geisler maintains, "theism . . . is a logical prerequisite to Christianity."[12] After all, Christian theology need not interpret the meaning of God's attributes in impersonal and static ways, but can provide more adequate and appropriate interpretations of them. So, it is quite legitimate to defend theism in response to the problem of evil.

12. Norman Geisler, *Christian Apologetics* (Grand Rapids: Baker, 1976), preface.

The Classification of Evil

Upon facing the problem of evil as a serious and legitimate challenge to Christian belief, it might seem advisable to start with a precise definition of evil. However, the attempt to be specific at this point frequently ladens the meaning of evil with one's own perspective and thus hinders objective discussion. For example, some thinkers define evil in theological terms as "sin" and consider the problem only in this light, reducing all evils to spiritual rebellion and its consequences. Other thinkers define evil as "finitude" and then treat all evil—even human perversity—as the inevitable results of limitation. Definitions of evil could be proposed and debated indefinitely. Therefore, it is advisable for present purposes to leave open the question of definition and proceed with a broad, commonsense notion of evil. Regardless of how we define evil, we are all aware of its existence and profusion. It is entirely possible to identify a whole spectrum of events and experiences as evil without settling on some final definition. The set of commonly recognized evils includes, at the very least, such things as extreme pain and suffering, physical deformities, psychological abnormalities, the prosperity of bad men, the demise of good men, disrupted social relations, unfulfilled potential, a host of character defects, and natural catastrophes. What this list does, in philosophical parlance, is to begin to locate the *extension* (i.e., particular applications) of the term *evil* without specifying its exact *intension* (i.e., meaning).

Evil indeed has many faces, faces with which we are all too familiar. It is standard to distinguish between *moral* and *natural* evils, and thereby introduce a measure of order into the myriad evils we experience. This distinction performs a helpful classificatory function, although there is occasional disagreement over what items to include in the two categories. The distinction also allows us to divide the general problem of evil into the subsidiary problems of moral and natural evil, and thus guides further stages of inquiry.

Let us consider some familiar proposals. Alvin Plantinga writes:

> We must distinguish between *moral evil* and *natural evil*. The former is evil which results from free human activity; natural evil is any other kind of evil.[13]

As Plantinga admits, the distinction is not very precise. Yet this same point is made by John Hick:

> Moral evil is evil that we human beings originate: cruel, unjust, vicious, and perverse thoughts and deeds. Natural evil is the evil that originates independently of human actions: in disease bacilli, earthquakes, storms, droughts, tornadoes, etc.[14]

Edward Madden and Peter Hare provide a similar classification:

> *Physical evil*, we shall say, denotes the terrible pain, suffering, and untimely death caused by events like fire, flood, landslide, hurricane, earthquake, tidal wave, and famine and by diseases like cancer, leprosy, and tetanus—as well as the crippling defects and deformities like blindness, deafness, dumbness, shrivelled limbs, and insanity by which so many sentient beings are cheated of the full benefits of life. ... *Moral evil* ... denotes both moral wrong-doing such as lying, cheating, stealing, torturing,

13. Alvin Plantinga, *God, Freedom, and Evil* (Grand Rapids: Eerdmans, 1977), p. 30.

14. John Hick, *Evil and the God of Love*, rev. ed. (New York: Harper and Row, 1975), p. 12.

and murdering and character defects like greed, deceit, cruelty, wantonness, cowardice, and selfishness.[15]

Other authors do not depart far from this general approach to the distinction.

It seems that both Plantinga and Hick overextend the category of moral evil to cover even the pain one suffers as a result of another's wrongful action. Furthermore, it appears that Madden and Hare overrestrict the category of natural evil to exclude physical effects which occur due to human initiative. Would it not be better to resolve this ambiguity by recognizing that in some cases there are *complex* evils, such as a wrongful deed (or moral evil) and a painful condition (or natural evil) resulting from the deed? Actually, the human actions which cause some natural evils are not necessarily sinful or wrong, since much pain and suffering comes from accidental or inadvertent actions. Debate over the exact boundaries between natural and moral evils, an important distinction in clarifying our thinking about evil, could be continued indefinitely.

The Many Faces of Evil

The classification of evils is certainly an important and perhaps necessary step toward generating a response to the problem of evil. However, the task of classifying various evils, as well as the larger task of rationally responding to the distinct problems they pose, may seem to proceed at a distance from the concrete reality of evil. Although the problem of evil is, in a legitimate sense, abstract and theoretical, it is a problem about real evils which occur to real people. The disturbing theoretical questions arise when actual evils are viewed in light of

15. Edward Madden and Peter Hare, *Evil and the Concept of God* (Springfield, IL: Charles C. Thomas, 1968), p. 6.

Christian theism, which affirms that a God of power and grace superintends the world. Not being able to reconcile the evils of existence with the belief in this kind of God can even add to the psychological anguish which people experience. A brief survey of the panorama of disturbing evils will help us bear in mind the experiential basis of the problem.

For some, the existence of very terrible and widespread evils suggests that there is no God who loves and cares for all. For example, there are many who have drawn an atheistic conclusion from Auschwitz, as theologian Eugene Borowitz explains:

> Any God who could permit the Holocaust, who could remain silent during it, who could "hide His face" while it dragged on, was not worth believing in. There might well be a limit to how much we could understand about Him, but Auschwitz demanded an unreasonable suspension of understanding. In the face of such great evil, God, the good and the powerful, was too inexplicable, so men said "God is dead."[16]

The Holocaust is one of a long list of horrendous evils which seriously threaten (if they do not destroy) belief in God.

It is not always the dramatic, momentous evils which shake belief in God. On a smaller scale, it is frequently the innumerable common events and experiences of life which reveal the negative side of existence and make faith in God extremely difficult. Over a period of time, many evil events—bank robberies, even rapes—come to be accepted as routine or familiar. Contemporary journalism typically adopts a factual and objective style to report

16. Eugene Borowitz, *The Mask Jews Wear* (New York: Simon and Schuster, 1973), p. 99.

such tragedies. Notice the way in which *Time* magazine reported a needless infant death:

> In Manhattan, Nancy Alverson left her 2½ year-old daughter in their Greenwich Village apartment while she went shopping. Back in "a few minutes," she found the child dead of suffocation, with her head swathed in the adhering layers of a plastic garment bag.[17]

Also accepted as routine in the modern world are natural evils such as earthquakes, tidal waves, drought, starvation, and epidemics, which terrify, injure, and kill thousands upon thousands every year. No matter how routine various evils are taken to be, their cumulative effect on sensitive, thinking persons is frequently that of continual confirmation that this world, as well as whatever transworldly source it might have, is certainly not accommodated to human values.

When we move away from routine journalistic reports of evil and uncover more fully its marks on human life, the impact is, for some, overwhelming. In *Miss Lonelyhearts*, Nathanael West captures in vivid fashion the heartache and despair which are wrought in human life by blind physical events. Take this example from the beginning of the book:

> Dear Miss Lonelyhearts—
> I am sixteen years old now and I dont know what to do and would appreciate it if you could tell me what to do. When I was a little girl it was not so bad because I got used to the kids on the block makeing fun of me, but now I would like to have boy friends like the other girls and go out on Saturday nites, but no boy will take me because I was born without a nose—although I am a good

17. *Time,* 11 May 1959, p. 21.

dancer and have a nice shape and my father buys me pretty clothes.

I sit and look at myself all day and cry. I have a big hole in the middle of my face that scares people even myself so I cant blame the boys for not wanting to take me out. My mother loves me, but she crys terrible when she looks at me.

What did I do to deserve such a terrible bad fate? Even if I did do some bad things I didnt do any before I was a year old and I was born this way. I asked Papa and he says he doesnt know, but that maybe I did something in the other world before I was born or that maybe I was being punished for his sins. I dont believe that because he is a very nice man. Ought I commit suicide?

Sincerely yours,
Desperate[18]

"Desperate" is only one of a multitude of cases of intense human suffering and torment.

The celebrated eighteenth-century philosopher, David Hume, suggested that evils arising from our own human constitution are probably more frightful than any of the others. In his *Dialogues Concerning Natural Religion*, Demea, one of the disputants, makes this point after citing *Paradise Lost:*

Hear the pathetic enumeration of the great poet.
 Intestine stone and ulcer, colic-pangs,
 Demoniac frenzy, moping melancholy,
 And moon-struck madness, pining atrophy,
 Marasmus, and wide-wasting pestilence.
 Dire was the tossing, deep the groans: *Despair*
 Tended the sick, busiest from couch to couch.
 And over them triumphant *Death* his dart

---

18. Nathanael West, *Miss Lonelyhearts* in *The Complete Works of Nathanael West* (New York: Farrar, Straus, and Giroux, 1957), p. 43; the mistakes in this excerpt are intentional.

> Shook: but delay'd to strike, though oft invok'd
> With vows, as their chief good and final hope.

The disorders of the mind, continued Demea, though more secret, are not perhaps less dismal and vexatious. Remorse, shame, anguish, rage, disappointment, anxiety, fear, defection, despair—who has ever passed through life without inroads from these tormentors?[19]

There is no denying that men often fall victims to physical and psychological forces which are largely beyond their control.

Sometimes we fixate on the evils which persons suffer and undergo: a whole race is tortured, a woman is raped, a baby is fatally neglected. But the more subtle and terrifying side of evil must not be overlooked—its inextricable outworking in human thought and action. Persons not only undergo evil, but perform, inflict, and perpetrate evil. "Man's inhumanity to man," wrote Robert Burns, "makes countless thousands mourn." This personal aspect of evil most closely coincides with what the Bible describes as sin.

Fyodor Dostoevsky treats scornfully the comforting notion that man is always rational and good. In a famous passage from *The Brothers Karamazov* Dostoevsky protests such wild optimism about humankind:

> I can't endure that a man of lofty mind and heart begins with the ideal of the Madonna and ends with the ideal of Sodom. What's still more awful is that a man with the ideal of Sodom in his soul does not renounce the ideal of the Madonna, and his heart may be on fire with that ideal, genuinely on fire, just as in the days of youth and innocence.[20]

19. David Hume, *Dialogues Concerning Natural Religion*, ed. Henry D. Aiken (New York: Hafner, 1948), pp. 63–64.

20. Fyodor Dostoevsky, *The Brothers Karamazov*, trans. Constance Garnett (New York: Norton, 1976), p. 97.

The theme of the depravity and perversity of man is a recurrent one in great literature.

Robert Louis Stevenson vividly illustrates man's peculiar nature in his frightening fable of *Dr. Jekyll and Mr. Hyde*. The kind and decent Dr. Jekyll describes his discovery of the power of the transforming drug:

> It severed in me those provinces of good and ill which divide and compound man's dual nature. I was in no sense a hypocrite; both sides of me were in dead earnest; I was no more myself when I laid aside restraint and plunged in shame, than when I laboured, in the eye of day, at the furtherance of knowledge or the relief of sorrow and suffering.[21]

As time went on, the thought of evil no longer filled Jekyll with terror:

> I sat in the sun on a bench; the animal within me licking the chops of memory; the spiritual side a little drowsed, promising subsequent penitence, but not yet moved to begin. I began to be aware of the temper of my thoughts, a greater boldness, a contempt of danger, a solution of the bonds of obligation.[22]

The apelike creature had diabolically gained control of Jekyll:

> This was the shocking thing; that the slime of the pit seemed to utter cries and voices; that the amorphous dust gesticulated and sinned; that what was dead, and had no shape, should usurp the offices of life. And this again, that the insurgent horror was knit to him closer than a wife, closer than an eye; lay caged in his flesh, where he heard

21. Robert Louis Stevenson, *The Strange Case of Dr. Jekyll and Mr. Hyde* (London: The Folio Society, 1948), p. 124.
22. Ibid., p. 127.

it mutter and felt it struggle to be born; and at every hour of weakness, and in the confidence of slumber prevailed against him, and deposed him out of life.[23]

Dr. Jekyll confessed the terrible truth that he was radically both natures: "It was the curse of mankind that these incongruous fagots were thus bound together—that in the agonized womb of consciousness these polar twins should be continuously struggling."[24]

The apostle Paul recognized the war within himself between the spirit and the flesh: "I do not understand my own actions. For I do not do what I want, but I do the very thing I hate. . . . I can will what is right, but I cannot do it. For I do not do the good I want, but the evil I do not want is what I do."[25] Augustine unhappily gives a similar report in his *Confessions:* "I was bound, not with another's irons, but by my own iron will. My will the enemy held, and thence had made a chain for me, and bound me."[26]

To note the internal conflict in man, his paradoxical state, is not to affirm in a blanket way that man is totally depraved or worthless. Blaise Pascal, who knew well that man's passion is pitted against his reason and plunges him into discord and division, still proclaimed that "the greatness of a man is so evident that it is even proved by his wretchedness. For what in animals is nature in man we call wretchedness: by which we recognize that, his nature being now unlike that of animals, he has fallen from a better nature which was once his."[27]

Personal evil has collective as well as individual dimensions. Organized crime syndicates, militant nations,

23. Ibid., p. 146.
24. Ibid., pp. 124–25.
25. Paul's lamentation should be read in context: Romans 7:15–20.
26. Augustine, *Confessions*, 8. 5. 10.
27. Blaise Pascal, *Pensées*, no. 409.

oppressive social structures, and profit-crazed multinational corporations are, in a real sense, the social extensions of personal evil. On both individual and corporate levels, one of the saddest features of human evil is its strange admixture with good or apparent good. Marriages are wrecked for lack of mutual understanding, educational communities are undermined by disagreement about how to pursue common ideals, political parties are thrown into disarray by excessive ambition, and nations are ripped apart by struggles for power. There can be little doubt that the subtle human potential for evil is most horrifying. Out of the ancient past, the prophet Jeremiah issues the indictment: "The heart is deceitful above all things, and desperately corrupt; who can understand it?" (Jer. 17:9).

No list of evils can omit the pain which afflicts a large part of the animal world. As Alfred Lord Tennyson reminds us, nature is "red in tooth and claw." Survival of the fittest seems to be built into the mechanism of animate nature. Few animals are free from the threat of being attacked and devoured by stronger animals. And no "brute" is more insensitive and cruel than man, who overkills birds, deer, and other animals for sport, employs leghold traps which keep fur-bearing animals suffering for days, and clubs to death baby seals.

C. S. Lewis attempts to minimize the problem of animal pain by indicating that animals do not have self-aware souls which perceive the significance and continuity of their own painful states.[28] We can readily grant that animals are not equivalent to men in their levels of consciousness and depths of emotion. However, they obviously feel pain, endure suffering, and fear death. Therefore, the physical condition of these nonhuman creatures is a very

---

28. C. S. Lewis, *The Problem of Pain* (New York: Macmillan, 1962), pp. 129–43.

serious matter. It is a matter which again raises the question of whether this kind of evil (e.g., the threat of being attacked by stronger animals) could have been created by the God of the Christian faith. William Blake forms the question very forcefully in "The Tiger":

> Tiger! Tiger! burning bright
> In the forests of the night,
> What immortal hand or eye
> Could frame thy fearful symmetry?
>
> In what distant deeps or skies
> Burned the fire of thine eyes?
> On what wings dare he aspire?
> What the hand dare seize the fire?
>
> And what shoulder, and what art,
> Could twist the sinews of thy heart?
> And when thy heart began to beat,
> What dread hand? and what dread feet?
>
> What the hammer? what the chain?
> In what furnace was thy brain?
> What the anvil? what dread grasp
> Dare its deadly terrors clasp?
>
> When the stars threw down their spears,
> And watered heaven with their tears,
> Did he smile his work to see?
> Did he who made the Lamb make Thee?
>
> Tiger! Tiger! burning bright
> In the forests of the night,
> What immortal hand or eye
> Dare frame thy fearful symmetry?[29]

29. William Blake, "The Tiger," in *Eighteenth Century Poetry and Prose*, ed. Louis I. Bredvold et al., 2nd ed. (New York: Ronald Press, 1956), pp. 1060–61.

At the end of any catalogue of ills which plague the world comes death. And death is a particularly acute problem for the human species. Indeed death is the last enemy, the last evil we must face; it puts an end to our doing and undergoing further evils. Ludwig Wittgenstein observes: "Death is not an event in life: we do not live to experience death."[30] Death is the end of life. H. F. Lovell Cocks writes that the termination of one's own personal existence is the "great human repression, the universal 'complex.' Dying is the reality that man dare not face, and to escape which he summons all his resources."[31]

Noel Coward's comedy *This Happy Breed* illustrates the uneasiness and embarrassment we encounter when talking about this forbidden subject. Frank and his sister Sylvia, who is a fervent Christian Scientist neophyte, are conversing in the lounge after supper. Ethel, Frank's wife, is in the kitchen:

Sylvia: There's not so much to do since Mrs. Flint passed on.

Frank: I do wish you wouldn't talk like that, Sylvia, it sounds so soft.

Sylvia: I don't know what you mean, I'm sure.

Frank: (firmly) Mother died, see! First of all she got flu and that turned to pneumonia and the strain of that affected her heart, which was none too strong at the best of times, and she DIED. Nothing to do with passing on at all.

Sylvia: How do you know?

Frank: I admit it's only your new way of talking, but it gets me down, see?

(Ethel comes in)

Ethel: What are you shouting about?

30. Ludwig Wittgenstein, *Tractatus Logico-Philosophicus*, trans. D. F. Pears and B. F. McGuinness (London: Routledge and Kegan Paul, 1971), proposition 6.4311, p. 147.

31. H. F. Lovell Cocks, *By Faith Alone* (London: James Clarke, 1943), p. 55.

Frank: I'm not shouting about anything at all. I'm merely explaining to Sylvia that mother died. She didn't pass on or pass over or pass out—she DIED.[32]

Not only Christian Scientists deny the fact of physical death. Our general society glosses over the ultimacy of death.

Until very recently, contemporary culture has tried to keep its children from "the facts of death" while anxiously exposing them to "the facts of life." It is almost pornographic how death has been covered over with elaborate cosmetic devices and surrounded by a wealth of extravagant detail. In *The High Cost of Dying*, Ruth Mulvey Harmer sarcastically describes the elaborate measures of funeral parlors:

> The body is no longer a corpse; it is the "departed," the "loved one," or even—with greater liveliness— "Mr. . . . . . ." And "Mr. . . . . ." is no longer "laid out" for viewing; if he is not actually stretched out on a bed in a "reposing room," he is in the "slumber room" waiting to greet visitors, with his nails carefully manicured, the proper make-up applied, and perhaps holding a pipe or a book in a remarkably "natural" way. . . . Coffins have become caskets to hold a precious treasure. . . . More recently, they have become "couches" to banish further all thoughts of death.[33]

Death and dying is gradually becoming an accepted topic for study and discussion. The increased frankness about death seems to be showing up such funeral-parlor games for what they are—frightened but shallow attempts to cover up the way we all must end.

32. Noel Coward, *This Happy Breed* (New York: Doubleday, 1947), Act 3, Scene 1, p. 178.

33. Ruth Mulvey Harmer, *The High Cost of Dying* (New York: Collier, 1963), p. 19.

While much newly found openness toward these topics has produced beneficial results, it has also spawned opposite methods for minimizing death. For example, Elisabeth Kübler-Ross explains and normalizes death as the next stage of human development or the "final stage of growth."[34] In the words of Raymond Moody, there is even proof of "life after life."[35] These "proofs," which are composed largely of accumulated firsthand reports by persons who were temporarily pronounced clinically dead, typically portray a kind of palatable afterlife which is entered rather automatically at death. The natural immortality of the soul is simply assumed without careful analysis and argument. Although these new developments in modern thanatology distinguish themselves from the methods of jaded funeral-parlor cosmetology, the net results are the same: death is naturalized and made more easily acceptable.

Without rehearsing here all of the defects of contemporary approaches to death,[36] we simply must note the contrast to the words of Jesus: "I am the resurrection and the life; he who believes in me, though he die, yet shall he live" (John 11:25). Christian theology cuts sharply against the ambiguous life-after-life mentality and affirms that death is *not* natural. It is radically foreign to all that is within us. It is the last enemy which must be overcome. Those who have thought long and hard about the human

34. Elisabeth Kübler-Ross, *Death: The Final Stage of Growth* (Englewood Cliffs, NJ: Prentice-Hall, 1975).

35. Raymond A. Moody, Jr., *Life After Life* (New York: Bantam, 1975).

36. Among the most serious defects of the life-after-life movement are the following: First, it confuses the relation between empirical science and metaphysics, and proceeds as though the former could prove or disprove the theses of the latter, such as survival after bodily death. Second, it too readily forgets the tentative and relative nature of scientific tests, particularly those for physical death. Third, it almost uncritically concludes that the collected reports deal with events which occurred during death; it does not fully explore the possibilities that these are reports of hallucinations or dreams (or whatever) which occurred near death.

condition and refuse to settle for the cheap and easy talk about personal survival know this already. Death, then, is another forceful evidence of the problem of evil.

We can now begin to see more clearly why evil is indeed, as Hans Küng says, "the rock of atheism."[37] The persistence of evil is an inescapable fact of human history. In the experience of evil and reflection upon it, mankind reaches the extreme limit—the decisive question of the meaning of life, of the sense and nonsense of reality. Therefore, the Christian view of human existence faces its most serious test when applied to the presence of evil in the world.

37. Hans Küng, *On Being a Christian*, trans. Edward Quinn (Garden City, NY: Doubleday, 1976), p. 432.

2

Evil and Inconsistency

A Setting for the Problem of Evil

In Fyodor Dostoevsky's *Brothers Karamazov* the reunion of Ivan and Alyosha Karamazov, long separated by the odysseys of their different lives, provides poignant expression of the problem before us. Ivan, a university-educated and worldly-wise man turned atheist, seeks to elicit an answer to the evils of life from Alyosha, who has become a faithful monk:

> By the way, a Bulgarian I met lately in Moscow . . . told me about the crimes committed by the Turks and Circassians in all parts of Bulgaria through fear of a general rising of the Slavs. They burn villages, murder, rape women and children, they nail their prisoners to the fences by the ears, leave them so till morning, and in the morning they hang them—all sorts of things you can't imagine. People talk sometimes of bestial cruelty, but that's a great injustice and insult to the beast; a beast can never be so cruel as a man, so artistically cruel. The tiger only tears and gnaws, that's all he can do.[1]

1. Fyodor Dostoevsky, *The Brothers Karamazov*, trans. Constance Garnett (New York: Norton, 1976), p. 219. This encounter of Ivan and Alyosha constitutes one of the high points of world literature and deserves careful reading (Book Five, "Pro and Contra," chapters 3–5).

Ivan reveals that he collects stories of such evils, particularly those of the suffering of innocent children. His point is that God—Alyosha's God—is supposed to be mighty and just, but that the world is full of absurdity and injustice, pain and suffering.

Ivan insists that he cannot commit his life to a system of religious beliefs which fails so utterly to make sense of life:

> With my pitiful, earthly, Euclidean understanding, all I know is that there are none guilty; that cause follows effect, simply and directly; that everything flows and finds its level—but that's only Euclidean nonsense, I know that, and I can't consent to live by it![2]

And even if it were promised that there will be a future harmony, divinely wrought, the cost is too dear:

> I understand, of course, what an upheaval of the universe it will be, when everything in heaven and earth blends in one hymn of praise and everything that lives and has lived cries aloud: "Thou art just, O Lord, for thy ways are revealed." . . . [But] I don't want to cry aloud then. While there is still time, I hasten to protect myself and so I renounce the higher harmony altogether. . . . I would rather be left with the unavenged suffering. . . . Besides, too high a price is asked for such harmony; it's beyond our means to pay so much to enter on it. And so I hasten to give back my entrance ticket, and if I am an honest man I am bound to give it back as soon as possible. And that I am doing. It's not God that I don't accept, Alyosha, only I most respectfully return Him the ticket.[3]

Alyosha is overwhelmed by Ivan's reasonings, and in desperation brings up the figure of Christ, hoping that it will

2. Ibid., p. 224.
3. Ibid., pp. 225–26.

satisfy Ivan. But Ivan meets his brother's attempt with a story he has prepared about Christ before the Grand Inquisitor.

In Ivan's "poem," God chooses once more to walk in human form among men:

> And behold, He deigned to appear for a moment to the people, to the tortured, suffering people, sunk in iniquity, but loving Him like children. My story is laid in Spain, in Seville, in the most terrible time of the Inquisition, when fires were lighted every day to the glory of God, and
>
> > In the splendid *auto da fé*
> > The wicked heretics were burnt.[4]

Ivan continues the narration with extraordinary passion and force:

> He came softly, unobserved, and yet, strange to say, everyone recognized Him. . . . He holds out His hands to them, blesses them, and a healing virtue comes from contact with Him, even with His garments.[5]

The crowd weeps and sings, "Hosannah!"

Following Him to the steps of the Seville cathedral, the people witness Him restore life to a dead girl, gently pronouncing once again the ancient words, "Maiden, arise." The ensuing scene is gripping:

> There are cries, sobs, confusion among the people, and at that moment the cardinal himself, the Grand Inquisitor, passes by the cathedral. He is an old man, almost ninety, tall and erect, with a withered face and sunken eyes, in which there is still a gleam of light, like a fiery spark. He is not dressed in his gorgeous cardinal's robes, as he was

4. Ibid., p. 229.
5. Ibid.

the day before, when he was burning the enemies of the Roman Church—at that moment he was wearing his coarse, old monk's cassock.[6]

The old cardinal, followed by a train of assistants and guards, sees everything. The cardinal's face darkens, he knits his brow, and quickly orders the guards to take the mysterious stranger. His power is so complete that the crowd bows in submission and immediately parts for the guards. The stern monk blesses the crowd in cold silence and passes on.

The prisoner is led to the shadowy, vaulted prison in the palace of the Holy Inquisition. That breathless night another inquisition takes place. The heavy iron door of the prison opens and the cardinal steps inside. The door is closed at once behind him, and he stands alone, light in hand, and gazes into the prisoner's face. At last, the cardinal speaks:

> "Is it Thou? Thou?" but receiving no answer, he adds at once, "Don't answer, be silent. What canst thou say, indeed? I know too well what thou wouldst say. And Thou hast no right to add anything to what Thou hadst said of old. Why, then, art Thou come to hinder us? For Thou hast come to hinder us, and Thou knowest that. But dost Thou know what will be tomorrow? I know not who Thou art and care not to know whether it is Thou or only a semblance of Him, but tomorrow I shall condemn Thee and burn Thee at the stake as the worst of heretics. And the very people who have today kissed Thy feet, tomorrow at the faintest sign from me will rush to heap up the embers of Thy fire."[7]

The aged cardinal continues, bemoaning the evils which are caused by man's misuse of God's gift of free will:

6. Ibid., p. 230.
7. Ibid., p. 231.

They will cry aloud at last that the truth is not in Thee,
for they could not have been left in greater confusion and
suffering than Thou hast caused, laying upon them so
many cares and unanswerable problems.[8]

The prisoner remains silent. Then comes the climax of
their encounter:

When the Inquisitor ceased speaking he waited some time
for his Prisoner to answer him. . . . But [the Prisoner] sud-
denly approached the old man in silence and softly kissed
him on his bloodless aged lips. That was all his answer.[9]

Alyosha heard Ivan's story to the end and then tried to
persuade him that its pessimism and despair are practically impossible. But Ivan's replies were too penetrating.
Unable to answer the thrust of Ivan's story, Alyosha stood
up and kissed Ivan gently on the lips. Alyosha turned and
ran back to the monastery. "It was nearly dark, and he
felt almost frightened."[10]

The deep feeling which Alyosha must have had upon
hearing Ivan's story is not to be minimized. However,
Alyosha's troubled behavior may be seen as all too typical
of religious reactions to the problem of evil when it is
powerfully articulated in real-life situations: *emotional
response, rational retreat*. It is quite normal for believers
to be disturbed by the evils of life and to sense their tendency to discourage or destroy religious faith. Unfortunately, many of these believers cannot offer reasons why
evil need not have such force. The problem of evil, then,
often becomes construed as an emotional matter.

However, the issue cannot be construed as completely
emotional. In this chapter, the emotional response to the

8. Ibid., pp. 235–36; also read 236–41.
9. Ibid., p. 243.
10. Ibid., p. 245.

problem of evil will be examined and found insufficient to meet the essence of Ivan's challenge. Then, we will press toward a way of understanding the problem of evil as a rational or theoretical difficulty. The theoretical dimension of the problem of evil will be seen to consist of two distinct versions: the logical argument and the evidential argument. Since the exact formulation one countenances influences the direction of his analysis, close attention will be given to each. The present chapter considers the logical version of the problem of evil; the next chapter focuses on the evidential version, clarifying the issue at stake in the rest of the book.

The Emotional Response to the Problem of Evil

It is not difficult to find authors who believe that the intellectual questions about evil are either unimportant or irrelevant. They prefer to treat the problem of evil as purely emotional, superseding rational considerations. For example, John Bowker writes in *Problems of Suffering in Religions of the World:*

> There is nothing theoretical or abstract about it. To talk of suffering is to talk not of an academic problem but of the sheer bloody agonies of existence, of which all men are aware and have direct experience. All religions take account of this; some, indeed, make it the basis of all they have to say. Whatever theoretical constructions may be built, the foundations are laid in the apparent realities of what it is like to be alive. Thus what a religion has to say about suffering reveals, in many ways, more than anything else, what it believes the nature and purpose of existence to be.[11]

11. John Bowker, *Problems of Suffering in Religions of the World* (New York: Cambridge University, 1970), p. 2.

Max Weber places strong emphasis on the psychological need of the individual to explain suffering and evil. The need arises from the discrepancy between, on one hand, normal human interests and expectations in any society, and, on the other, what actually happens. Commenting on Weber, Talcott Parsons says that the discrepancy generates "*ad hoc* elements of tension" and creates "experiences which are frustrating."[12] These existential factors may, in turn, stimulate some level of rationalization in the individual. But, at base, the problem of evil is still subjective and personal.

In his classic work, *The Varieties of Religious Experience*, William James treats the problem and its solution in terms of "inner attitude," not "systematic philosophy." The problem of evil is assuaged, as James says, by developing the proper attitude or "healthy-mindedness":

> Much of what we call evil is due entirely to the way men take the phenomenon. . . . Since you make [facts] evil or good by your own thoughts about them, it is the ruling of your thoughts which proves to be your principal concern.[13]

It is true that James does not take the problem of evil lightly, and at times seems to contradict this statement. Nevertheless, his statement represents a very attractive and widespread position.

A. R. King agrees that, although a theoretical structure can be contrived for the problem of evil, the problem is essentially an experiential matter. Generalizing from the case of Job, King emphasizes the distinction between hearsay about and the experience of God. He insists that,

12. Talcott Parsons, Introduction to Max Weber, *The Sociology of Religion*, trans. Ephraim Fischoff (Boston: Beacon Press, 1963), p. xlvii.

13. William James, *The Varieties of Religious Experience* (New York: Macmillan, 1961), p. 86.

since there may be no rational answer, the real solution
to evil is found in an existential encounter with God: "A
religious pragmatism and mysticism ... boldly affirms
the paradox and pursues the matter in terms of practical
adjustments to evil."[14]

Unfortunately, this kind of position is not without serious difficulties. When the problem of evil is defined as
a completely emotional one, it tends to reduce to a purely
psychological or practical matter. Proposed solutions, then,
can aim at little more than inducing certain subjective
states in oneself and others: resignation, hope, courage,
or whatever. When emotional considerations take prece-
dence over rational ones, spontaneous answers given in
the face of actual evils are usually fragmentary and in-
applicable, and ultimately become arbitrary and relative.

Obviously, the emotional aspects of the problem of evil
cannot be ignored or ridiculed; but neither can they be
treated as the primary problem. The classic and enduring
problem concerns the rational acceptability of Christian
belief in light of evil in the world, regardless of how different persons respond emotionally to the various evils
which they encounter. Moreover, adopting a certain rational understanding of evil may well determine which
attitudinal or emotional reactions are proper and helpful.
It can even be argued that any given emotional response
entails certain beliefs about evil. Of course, once this link-
age between conceptual commitment and subjective response is recognized, the personal domain of the problem
of evil can no longer be characterized as completely
emotional.

That aspect of the problem of evil which involves the
inward condition of the individual is best characterized
as existential. But the existential dimension of the prob-

14. Albion Roy King, *The Problem of Evil: Christian Concepts and the Book
of Job* (New York: Ronald Press, 1952), p. 213.

lem transcends pure emotion; it occurs as the total person seeks to relate himself to the whole realm of existence, a realm which contains the disturbing reality of evil. Since the total personal response to evil depends, in large part, upon the conceptual categories through which it is interpreted, consideration of the existential aspect must be postponed until the theoretical dimension is completely examined. In chapter 6, it will be shown that a full analysis of the evidential argument from gratuitous evil provides the proper theoretical basis for consideration of the existential sense of the problem of evil.

The Logical Version of the Problem of Evil

If the broadest division in the literature is between the existential and theoretical dimensions of the problem of evil, the next division is between the two major theoretical versions of the problem: the logical and evidential. We must now examine each one in turn, beginning with the logical problem[15] (also called the deductive problem[16] and the *a priori* problem[17]).

Thinkers who consider the logical problem take the issue to be whether basic Christian claims are inconsistent. Historically, the discussion of this problem is constituted by atheistic attempts to prove that certain propositions of Christian theism are inconsistent and theistic attempts to show why they are not. J. L. Mackie, for example, sums up the atheistic challenge: "Here it can be shown, not that religious beliefs lack rational support, but that they are

15. This term is also used by William Rowe, *Philosophy of Religion: An Introduction* (Belmont, CA: Dickenson, 1978), pp. 80–86.

16. See Michael L. Peterson, "Christian Theism and the Problem of Evil," *Journal of the Evangelical Theological Society* 21 (1978): 35–46.

17. See Alvin Plantinga, *God and Other Minds: A Study of the Rational Justification of Belief in God* (Ithaca, NY: Cornell University, 1967), p. 128.

positively irrational, that several parts of the essential theological doctrine are inconsistent with one another."[18]

We must begin by examining the general notion of logical inconsistency.[19] Technically speaking, two propositions are inconsistent when it is impossible for both of them to be true at the same time. This impossibility results when one proposition entails the denial of the other proposition. So, anyone who affirms both such propositions cannot be holding a position which is completely true. It is important to note that the issue of consistency is independent of the issue of truth or verification. Knowing the actual truth or falsity of the propositions in question is not required in order to ascertain whether they are logically consistent.

As a first example, take the person who accepts an explicit contradiction. Say the person believes both the proposition that

(a) Socrates is mortal

and the proposition that

(~a) Socrates is not mortal.

(The logical symbol ~ means the negation of a proposition.) Now what we have here is an instance of a person's adhering to a straightforward contradiction: (a) and (~a). Presumably, few people commit such flagrant errors in thinking.

However, some inconsistencies are not so obvious and thus more readily find acceptance. In these more difficult instances, the charge of inconsistency can still be made to

18. J. L. Mackie, "Evil and Omnipotence," *Mind* 64 (1955): 200.

19. For a more elaborate discussion of logical inconsistency, see Peter T. Manicas and Arthur N. Kruger, *Logic: The Essentials* (New York: McGraw-Hill, 1976), pp. 96–97, 106–08.

stick if a line of reasoning can be produced whereby the implicit inconsistency in some set of beliefs is made explicit.

As a second example, take the following set of beliefs in which there is a hidden inconsistency:

(b) All men are mortal;

(c) Socrates is a Greek;

(d) Socrates is a man;

(e) No Greeks are mortal.

Suppose that someone actually believed this set of four propositions. A critic would try to show that they all cannot be consistently held. The critic could demonstrate that, just beneath the surface of these propositions, there is a hidden logical contradiction. From (b) and (d) he can deduce

(a) Socrates is mortal.

But from (c) and (e) he can deduce

(~a) Socrates is not mortal.

So, the critic can show that one who accepts the set (b)–(e) is committed to both (a) and (~a), and thereby unwittingly embraces a logical contradiction. At least one of the propositions in the set (b)–(e) must then be rejected to escape the problem.

Admittedly, this example of an implicit contradiction is a simplified one; seldom do such easy cases occur in ordinary life. In real life, the matter is usually much more complex. Sometimes the propositions which form a contradiction in an opponent's position are not stated. So, the critic is faced with the double task of first producing all of the relevant unstated propositions and then drawing out the contradiction from the fully stated position.

An example which exhibits this procedure can be obtained by modifying the previous one. Suppose that a person believes propositions (b), (c), and (e). Then, for a critic to deduce a contradiction he would have to specify additional propositions which the person in question also believes or could be made to admit. The critic might take it that this person believes proposition (d) or that he really should be committed to (d) on some grounds or other. When it is shown that the person is or ought to be committed to (d) as well as to the original set (b), (c), and (e), the contradiction is forthcoming once again.

Now we can begin to investigate the atheistic challenge that evil can be used to establish that Christian theism is a system of inconsistent beliefs. Essentially, the challenge of the logical version of the problem of evil is that there is at least one contradiction derivable from theistic propositions about God and evil. The atheist must then prove this accusation. But the proof of inconsistency is not as easily accomplished as in the first example, for serious theists are not in the habit of holding patent contradictions. Neither does it appear that the atheist's task is going to be as easy as in the second example in which an implicit contradiction is derived from a stated set of propositions, since theists do not explicitly adhere to all of the propositions needed to deduce a contradiction. So, at best, the atheist must supplement the basic propositions of theism with additional propositions to which the theist is presumably committed and then try to deduce the fatal contradiction. But this task is much more difficult than it appears in our simplified third example.

The whole issue over logical inconsistency rests on subtle and debatable interpretations of various Christian beliefs about the character of God, the meaning of evil, the nature of moral obligation, and a number of other matters. This complicates the issue beyond any neat and easy logical maneuver. Yet there are a number of atheists who are convinced that subterranean logical difficulties do exist for Christian theism, and who labor vigorously to excavate them. Likewise, there are a number of theists who take the matter of logical consistency seriously and work diligently to defend against these atheistic attacks.

The Structure of the Logical Problem

The atheist's basic task is to demonstrate how the essential claims of Christian theism, including claims about evil, are actually inconsistent. According to Alvin Plantinga, the atheist cannot be successful unless he identifies a set of propositions which both entails a contradiction and is such that each proposition in the set is either necessarily true, essential to theism, or a consequence of such propositions.[20] There is no logical problem if the Christian theist is not committed to each proposition in the set or if the set does not really entail a contradiction.

Atheistic philosophers have not differed significantly over the set of Christian claims which contains the rumored contradiction. Several propositions about God are frequently cited:

(1) God exists;

(2) God is omnipotent;

(3) God is omniscient;

(4) God is wholly good.

For brevity and clarity, the theistic position expressed above can be abbreviated in one complex proposition:

20. Plantinga, *God and Other Minds*, p. 117.

(G) An omnipotent, omniscient, wholly good God exists.

Any question about (G) is equivalent, then, to a question about one or more of the propositions which are condensed into it. The following analysis will focus on the issue between atheists who advance the charge of inconsistency and those theists who refuse to give up (G) or any of its constituent propositions (1)–(4) to escape the charge. Such defenders qualify as true theists, whereas those who relinquish or modify (G) are actually quasi theists.[21]

The logical version of the problem of evil is not completely formed until another proposition, one about evil, is introduced. It is this additional proposition which is allegedly inconsistent with (G). In the scholarship, three different propositions about evil have been proposed, each one determining a different formulation of the logical problem. Depending on how the atheist understands theism, he may formulate an argument to the effect that (G) is inconsistent with any *one* of the three following propositions about evil:

(E$_1$) Evil exists;

(E$_2$) Large amounts, extreme kinds, and perplexing distributions of evil exist;

(E$_3$) Gratuitous or pointless evil exists.

Figure 1 is a classificatory chart representing the different logical arguments based on these propositions. All of these arguments from evil are the same in that their structure is purely deductive and their strategy is to derive a contradiction from key theistic claims.

Atheistic critics of Christian theism have typically

---

21. This terminology is borrowed from Edward Madden and Peter Hare, *Evil and the Concept of God* (Springfield, IL: Charles C. Thomas, 1968).

Figure 1
Logical Arguments from Evil

I	II	III
(G)	(G)	(G)
is inconsistent	is inconsistent	is inconsistent
with	with	with
(E_1)	(E_2)	(E_3)

thought that formulation I is the most significant of the three approaches and the most likely to defeat theism. Hence, formulation I will be taken as the prime representative of the logical arguments from evil and treated in detail. Most of the analysis of formulation I applies *mutatis mutandis* to formulations II and III.

Statements of the classic logical problem designated by formulation I are not hard to find in the vast literature on God and evil. Two centuries ago, David Hume (after Epicurus) posed the problem in stark clarity:

> Is [God] willing to prevent evil, but not able? Then he is impotent. Is he able, but not willing? Then he is malevolent. Is he both able and willing? Whence then is evil?[22]

More recently, H. J. McCloskey stated the enigma:

> The problem of evil is a very simple one to state. There is evil in the world; yet the world is said to be the creation of a good and omnipotent God. How is this possible?

22. David Hume, *Dialogues Concerning Natural Religion*, ed. Henry D. Aiken (New York: Hafner, 1948), p. 66.

Surely a good omnipotent God would have made a world free of evil of any kind.[23]

Perhaps J. L. Mackie's rendition of the logical dilemma of the theist is clearest:

> In its simplest form the problem is this: God is omnipotent; God is wholly good; and yet evil exists. There seems to be some contradiction between these three propositions, so that if any two of them were true the third would be false. But at the same time all three are essential parts of most theological positions; the theologian, it seems, at once *must* adhere and *cannot consistently* adhere to all three.[24]

Statements of the logical problem could be continued indefinitely, but their point would still be the same.

The point of all such arguments is that the theist believes in the existence and perfection of God, and the atheist understands this belief to imply that there is no evil in the world. Yet the theist also believes that there is indeed evil in the world. Hence it seems to the atheistic critic that the theist's position is in serious internal difficulty. Casting the difficulty in terms of the precise propositions involved, we have the following logical situation. The theist is officially committed to:

> (G) An omnipotent, omniscient, wholly good God exists

and

> (E₁) Evil exists.

23. H. J. McCloskey, "The Problem of Evil," *Journal of Bible and Religion* 30 (1962): 187.
24. Mackie, "Evil," p. 200.

However, it appears to the atheistic critic that proposition (G) entails:

($\sim E_1$) Evil does not exist.

Now if (G) does entail ($\sim E_1$), then the theist is implicitly committed to ($\sim E_1$) as well. But this means that he is inconsistent because both (E_1) and ($\sim E_1$) figure into his theological position. To vindicate himself rationally, the theist must clarify and reconcile the propositions which supposedly generate the dread contradiction.

Propositions (G) and (E_1) are reasonably easy to reconcile as they stand, since (G) does not straightforwardly imply ($\sim E_1$). Hence, those who engage the logical version of the problem of evil quickly proceed to a different level of debate. It is commonly agreed that the alleged contradiction does not appear immediately on the face of (G) and (E_1). If the contradiction is there, it is implicit and must be made explicit by conjoining certain additional propositions to (G) and (E_1). And, to play fairly, the atheist must use propositions which the theistic position includes or propositions which are necessarily true for any position. The following are representative of the additional propositions often cited by the atheist:

(1') God is an independent being;

(2') God can perform any logically possible action, including the elimination of evil;

(3') God knows everything, including how to eliminate evil;

(4') God always seeks to promote good and eliminate evil;

(5') Evil is not logically necessary.

Now, from (G) and (1')–(5') it follows that

($\sim E_1$) Evil does not exist,

which does contradict (E_1). Alas, the atheist seems to have made good his charge of inconsistency by deriving from the theist's position two logically incompatible propositions: (E_1) and ($\sim E_1$). Obviously, by the law of noncontradiction, these two propositions cannot both be true at the same time and in the same sense. Hence, anyone holding them is irrational.

The reasoning behind this indictment is not hard to grasp. Christian theists say that God exists and has a definite character. It is natural to presume that God's character can be used as a basis for explaining (and perhaps predicting) His actions. Regarding the problem of evil, the divine attributes cited in (1)–(4) seem to have specifiable meanings which are delineated in the additional propositions (1')–(4'): if God is omnipotent, then He has the power to eliminate all evil, and so forth. According to the atheist, the conclusion of this type of reasoning seems to be that evil does not exist. However, evil does exist and its existence is recognized by the theist. Further, there is no logical necessity that evil exist, as indicated by (5'). The classic problem is thus forged out of what it seems that God would do about evil in the world.

Atheistic attacks which follow this general line of reasoning are plentiful. For example, J. L. Mackie sets forth propositions very much like (2') and (4') in order to expose the hidden inconsistency within Christian theism.[25] Another example is Richard LaCroix, who insists that many more statements are needed to convict theism of inconsistency, including statements to the effect that God Him-

25. Ibid., p. 201.

self is the greatest possible good and that He created freely.[26]

It must be remembered that it is characteristic of the logical version of the problem of evil to generate or attempt to generate an inconsistency from essential elements of theism. Otherwise it would not be possible to accuse the theist of inconsistency. The challenger might indeed find a set of propositions which involve a logical contradiction, but doing so is irrelevant unless they are central to theism. As we have seen, if the atheist cannot extract a contradiction from standard and familiar theistic propositions, he must use auxiliary propositions to which the theist must somehow be committed. This is precisely the point on which the atheistic attempts founder. Atheistic opponents have typically used one or more additional propositions which are not accepted by Christian theists.

Toward a Rebuttal of the Logical Version of the Problem

To recognize that the logical version of the problem relies on dubious assumptions is to focus on the exact point at which Christian thinkers must begin their rebuttal: they must show that one or more of the additional propositions are questionable and need not be accepted by the Christian theist. In effect, this is what orthodox theists have done throughout the history of theodicy. Augustine and Gottfried Leibniz argue that any additional proposition like (5') is false because any created finite world necessarily involves some evil.[27] According to them, if evil is logically necessary, God cannot remove it and

26. Richard R. LaCroix, "Unjustified Evil and God's Choice," *Sophia* 13 (1974): 20–28.

27. Augustine's mature views on this may be found in *The City of God*; Leibniz's position is contained in his *Theodicy*.

thus is not culpable. C. S. Lewis and M. B. Ahern maintain that propositions such as (4') do not hold because perfect goodness might have sufficient reasons for allowing some evil.[28] As Lewis puts it, God's goodness and love are much more "stern and splendid" than what (4') entails. Spanning the centuries from Augustine to Plantinga, the classic and most popular rationale for God's permission of evil is man's free will.[29] The theory is that God gave man free will and with it the possibility of both good and evil. Hence, God cannot eliminate evil without somehow curtailing or eliminating human freedom.

The vigorous theistic resistance to one or more of the propositions in the set (1')–(5') shows that the atheistic challenger is trying to palm off certain highly debatable propositions as integral to Christian theism. The atheistic case, of course, is that the theistic position is inconsistent, and thus that the theist is irrational. To make the charge stick, the atheist incorporates into the argument propositions which are not necessary to Christian theism. This amounts to nothing more than foisting on the theist propositions which he allegedly should believe and then handily exposing the contradiction in those beliefs. Instead the atheist should attempt to understand precisely what the theist really believes about God and evil. Otherwise the atheistic challenger may be forever doomed to repeat either of two fallacies when trying to deduce a contradiction within Christian theism: either *begging the question* by selecting propositions to which the theist is not committed, or *lifting out of context* propositions to which the theist is committed, but imputing new and convenient

28. C. S. Lewis, *The Problem of Pain* (New York: Macmillan, 1962), pp. 47–54; M. B. Ahern, *The Problem of Evil* (London: Routledge and Kegan Paul, 1971), p. 2.

29. Augustine, *The City of God;* Alvin Plantinga, *God, Freedom, and Evil* (Grand Rapids: Eerdmans, 1977).

meanings to them.[30] Both of these fallacies occur frequently in the literature on God and evil.

The preceding analysis shows that (G) and (E_1) are entirely consistent. Inconsistency seems to occur only when illicit assumptions are made about the meanings of (G) and (E_1). When the atheistic challenger makes such assumptions, he claims that it is *impossible* for both (G) and (E_1) to be true; that is, he claims that they are inconsistent. To defend the consistency of these propositions, the theist simply needs to show that it is *possible* for them both to be true. However, the theistic defender does not have to show that (G) and (E_1) are *true* or even *probably true*. What the theist must do is to show why repeated atheistic attempts to demonstrate inconsistency fail and why God could have some legitimate purposes for evil. This same strategy applies to the rebuttal of all of the different formulations of the logical argument from evil.

Variant Renditions of the Logical Problem

Actually, there is not just one formulation of the logical version of the problem of evil, but a cluster of different formulations. The force of these formulations in general should not be underestimated. It is somewhat curious, then, that the specific formulation (formulation I) discussed above receives so much attention. Formulation I purports to show that the theist's belief in the sheer existence of evil (i.e., just any evil at all) is somehow logically problematic within the context of his other theistic commitments. But in some ways this approach seems to be the weakest formulation of the logical argument from evil. The argument would be convenient for the atheist if

30. These syndromic errors are exposed in Michael L. Peterson, "Christian Theism and the Problem of Evil"; idem, "Evil and Inconsistency," *Sophia* 18 (1979): 20–27, which is a reply to LaCroix's version of the logical argument.

it did hold, but it is probably the easiest for the theist to rebut.

Perhaps this is why some authors have examined other formulations of the logical argument which are based on other theistic beliefs about evil. As depicted in Figure 1, there are two alternative formulations of the logical argument which might promise a more successful attack on Christian theism than the first one. Formulation II expresses the accusation that (G) is inconsistent with:

(E$_2$) Large amounts, extreme kinds, and perplexing distributions of evil exist.

Formulation III expresses the charge that (G) is inconsistent with:

(E$_3$) Gratuitous or pointless evil exists.

Although neither of these two formulations of the logical argument appears as often as the first, there are instances of them in the scholarly literature. To complete our discussion of the logical version of the problem of evil, these other formulations must be briefly analyzed.

Alvin Plantinga is aware that the atheistic challenger might offer an argument like formulation II:

The world, after all, contains a *great deal* of moral evil; and what we've seen so far is only that God's existence is compatible with *some* moral evil. Perhaps the atheologian can regroup; perhaps he can argue that at any rate God's existence is not consistent with the vast *amount* and *variety* of moral evil the universe actually contains.[31]

The essential challenge here is that proposition (G) is logically incompatible with proposition (E$_2$). The atheist is

31. Plantinga, *God, Freedom, and Evil*, p. 55.

deducing two propositions from theistic commitments: one stating that there are amounts, kinds, and distributions of evil which God would not allow, and one indicating that those amounts, kinds, and distributions do exist. This would reveal a contradiction.

But atheists have not been successful in their attempt to show that theists hold beliefs which either state or imply both that God limits the evil in the world and that those amounts, kinds, and distributions of evil He will allow have been exceeded. The proper theistic response seems to be to refuse to fix a limit on what evils God might allow. The theist can argue that it is entirely possible that God could countenance very extreme evils for a number of different reasons; for example, to preserve free will or to allow the regular operation of nature.

Another rendition of the problem of logical inconsistency corresponds to formulation III on the chart. Terence Penelhum argues that "it is logically inconsistent for a theist to admit the existence of a pointless evil."[32] In the terminology of formulation III, the theist is guilty of a logical contradiction if he believes that both (G) and (E_3) are true. The atheistic strategy required here is now quite familiar. It must be proved that the theist is unwittingly committed to the belief that God would not allow gratuitous evil *and* to the belief that gratuitous evil exists. The assumption of the atheist here is that theism recognizes the existence of even very severe evils as long as they have some point or meaning.

Certain stock theistic responses will also suffice to refute formulation III. The theist can take a traditional approach and argue that he is not really committed to (E_3). He can argue that there must be good explanations for all

32. Terence Penelhum, "Divine Goodness and the Problem of Evil," *Religious Studies* 2 (1966), reprinted in *Readings in the Philosophy of Religion: An Analytic Approach*, ed. Baruch Brody (Englewood Cliffs, NJ: Prentice-Hall, 1974), p. 226.

evils, no matter how severe, and hence that they cannot be meaningless. He might even venture some explanation, or range of explanations, designed to cover particularly troublesome evils.

Or, if the theist does accept (E_3), he can seek to point out that the additional assumptions which the atheist employs to derive the contradiction are not essential to theism and thus are unacceptable. The theist would argue that the logic of (G) leaves open the possibility that God might allow gratuitous evil. At first glance, this line of thinking may seem odd or perhaps unorthodox. However, a case can be made to show that it is entirely consistent with—indeed, is implied by—one valid interpretation of Christian theism.

Whether theism can involve a belief in the possibility of gratuitous evil is a question crucial to analysis of the third formulation of the logical problem and to an important corresponding formulation of the evidential problem. In fact, the controversy over gratuitous evil becomes intense in connection with the evidential problem.

In the final analysis, the logical version of the problem of evil does not seem to be a promising avenue of attack against Christian theism. Ironically, the atheistic challenger begins by accusing the theist of committing a logical mistake and ends up being embroiled in logical fallacies himself. Although formulation I is by far the most popular, it appears no more effective than the other two formulations. All of the formulations of the argument exhibit certain syndromic errors by attributing spurious propositions to theism. However, this does not preclude all prospects of there being a viable atheistic argument from evil. The current scholarship contains a growing number of *evidential* arguments from evil. These arguments constitute a mounting challenge which must now be examined.

3

Evil, Evidence, and God

Evil as Evidence Against Theism

In the current literature on God and evil, the evidential version of the problem of evil is gaining increased attention.[1] This version of the problem is alternatively called the inductive,[2] the *a posteriori*,[3] and the probabilistic[4] problem of evil. Each different designation suggests a slightly different way of understanding the problem; of these designations the term *evidential* best represents the type of argument from evil which this chapter examines. Unlike the logical version of the problem of evil, which seeks to show that Christian theism is internally *inconsistent*, the evidential version purports that, given the facts of evil, theism is *improbable*. Essentially, theism is treated as a highly general explanatory scheme which can be con-

1. This term is also used by William Rowe, *Philosophy of Religion: An Introduction* (Belmont, CA: Dickenson, 1978), p. 86.
2. See Michael L. Peterson, "Christian Theism and the Problem of Evil," *Journal of the Evangelical Theological Society* 21 (1978): 35–46; Bruce Reichenbach, "The Inductive Argument from Evil," *American Philosophical Quarterly* 17 (1980): 221–27.
3. See Alvin Plantinga, *God and Other Minds: A Study of the Rational Justification of Belief in God* (Ithaca, NY: Cornell University, 1967), p. 128.
4. See Alvin Plantinga, "The Probabilistic Argument from Evil," *Philosophical Studies* 35 (1979): 1–53.

firmed or disconfirmed according to relevant evidence. Evil is cited, then, as strong negative evidence against theism. In this way, rational grounds are provided for believing that theism is unlikely or implausible.

Almost automatically, the terms *evidence* and *probability* conjure up a picture of the methods of science. However, the problem of evil is not a scientific matter, but a philosophical and theological one. Therefore, the present use of terms such as "evidence," "probability," and the like is not exclusively scientific or mathematical; it is the same use these terms are given in rational discussion generally. Such terms occur in legal and moral reasoning,[5] and in philosophical dialectic.[6] Nor is there any oddity in employing them in the rational appraisal of religion.

While the evidential assessment of theological claims is not to be equated with the evidential assessment of scientific claims, it does bear certain analogies to the inductive treatment of hypotheses in science. Just as a general physical theory offers an explanation of certain manifest and pervasive features of the natural world, a theological framework provides an explanation of important types of events and experiences in the moral and spiritual realms. When an explanatory scheme appears to make good sense of the relevant facts, it is confirmed to that extent; when a conceptual scheme seems to fail to make sense of the pertinent facts, it is disconfirmed proportionately. The facts in question, then, serve as evidence for or against the theoretical understanding which is offered. Now there is no easy way to calculate the extent to which a given theoretical framework is made rationally acceptable or unacceptable by the available evidence, and this is no less true in theology than in science. Yet we still ascribe to theological claims some sense of probability or

5. Jonathan Cohen, *The Probable and the Provable* (Oxford: Clarendon Press, 1977).
6. Mortimer J. Adler, *The Conditions of Philosophy* (New York: Dell, 1967).

likelihood and seem to get along fairly well doing so. This indicates that there is a qualitative or rational measure of probability which is distinct from purely quantitative ones.

In view of the similarity between the evidential argument from evil and familiar modes of scientific reasoning, the following section employs the latter to elucidate the former. Relatively simplified models of confirmation and disconfirmation in science will be used to shed light on the strategy of the increasingly important evidential version of the problem of evil. Care must be taken not to claim too much for this method of comparison, for there are some dissimilarities which can be adduced. Nevertheless, the scientific process of confirmation or disconfirmation is rooted in basic rational procedures and thus bears significant resemblance to reasoning in other areas of intellectual concern, including theology and religion.

Obviously, one must be clear on the structure of the evidential argument from evil before one can effectively respond to it. However, this argument is not the only consideration in the overall evaluation of Christian theism. There are historical and existential arguments as well, many of which actually support theism. Thus, the complete rational appraisal of theism quickly becomes involved with a number of matters in addition to the problem of evil. The conscientious reader must sort through this complex of issues in order to reach some final judgment. Even if one thinks that one has sufficient grounds for Christian commitment, one must still be open to reviewing all of the issues in order to gain better self-understanding and greater sensitivity to why others do not share that commitment. Likewise, if one does not adhere to Christian theism, then he must make sure that he is aware of as many of the relevant issues as possible and has not focused on one isolated reason for his rejection of it. In this manner, all parties interested in the evaluation of theism can keep the question in proper perspective.

Interestingly, various thinkers who are equally cognizant of the theistic issues may weight them in different ways and, consequently, arrive at divergent conclusions. Exploring the causes of these differences can yield fascinating results bearing on epistemology and the theory of rationality. Without estimating here the exact weight which the problem of evil carries, one point is quite clear: for many, this problem is extremely important, and, for some, it is decisive. The remainder of this book, therefore, is devoted to formulating a response to the very formidable evidential version of the problem of evil, a response which, all things considered, may help tip the scales in favor of Christian theism.

The Nature of Evidential Reasoning

The type of reasoning involved in the evidential argument from evil is, broadly speaking, inductive. There are, of course, several approaches associated with induction, but the one operative in this argument is typically called inductive disconfirmation.[7] This is a strategy for showing that a given claim is falsified or made unacceptable by relevant factual statements. A similar approach is used to confirm hypotheses. After surveying both kinds of reasoning as they occur in science, we can further clarify the structure of the present theological issue over evil.

To begin, a few conventions and symbols must be adopted for the sake of precision and economy. For general purposes, a hypothesis shall be designated by the symbol (H) and its factual test by (T); an assumption shall

7. See Peter T. Manicas and Arthur N. Kruger, *Logic: The Essentials* (New York: McGraw-Hill, 1976), pp. 325–36; Carl Hempel, *Philosophy of Natural Science* (Englewood Cliffs, NJ: Prentice-Hall, 1966), pp. 7–9.

be denoted by (A). When citing a specific hypothesis, factual test, or assumption, we will use the same symbols, but in the lower case (h, t, a).

Consider first an example of confirmatory reasoning from the history of science. The hypothesis that

(h) The earth is spherical

was thought by Christopher Columbus to be partially confirmed by the factual test that

(t) The decks of receding ships always disappear from sight before their mastheads.

So, given the evidence cited in (t), (h) seems probable. Alternatively, (h) is taken to explain (t).

On the surface, the connection between (h) and (t) is very slim. What makes (t) confer such probability on (h) anyway? Modern philosophers of science indicate that any evidential test (T) must be connected or made relevant to a given hypothesis (H) by some additional assumptions (A). These assumptions may be derived from already confirmed and accepted hypotheses or may simply be granted for purposes of the investigation at hand. The key point is that they are already thought to be true, and hence their truth is not directly at stake. The function of these auxiliary assumptions is to make explicit just why a given (T) can be a test of a given (H). In terms of the present example, at least one additional assumption is needed:

(a) Light travels in straight lines.

Hence, from (h) and (a) we may say that it does clearly follow that (t) is true. And the occurrence (t) or nonoccurrence (~t) of the expected test result increases or decreases the probability of (h) accordingly.

Some logicians have tried to develop techniques for assigning precise numerical probability values to scientific propositions which are evaluated in this way.[8] However, these attempts have been successful only in limited kinds of cases. There is even more reason to believe that numerical probability values are inappropriate in philosophical theology.[9] Therefore, the rational or common-sense measures of probability (e.g., high, low, balanced, etc.) will be used in connection with the evidential argument from evil.

Because of its nondemonstrative or nondeductive character, inductive or evidential reasoning is probabilistic in the pertinent sense. There are three major factors which make the inductive evaluation of hypotheses probabilistic. Understanding these factors will, in turn, help us analyze the argument from evil which evaluates theism in somewhat analogous fashion.

The first factor involved in the probabilistic status of inductive thinking is its *a posteriori* character. Inductive reasoning depends upon at least one factual claim which must be verified through experience or observation. But experience or observation is always fallible and often incomplete. Hence, one could be mistaken about the occurrence of the relevant test results or might not be able to accumulate all of the evidence.

A second factor in the nondemonstrative or probabilistic nature of induction is the pattern of reasoning itself, which does not produce a conclusion with absolute certainty. In the case of confirmation (i.e., when the expected result occurs), induction involves what is called the deductive fallacy of affirming the consequent. Symbolically the general confirmation process (e.g., as used in the preceding spherical-earth vignette) looks like this:

8. Manicas and Kruger, *Logic*, pp. 264–82.
9. See Plantinga, "The Probabilistic Argument from Evil."

1. If (H) is true, then, assuming (A) is true, (T) will be true.
2. <u>(T) appears to be true.</u>
3. Therefore, (H) is probably true.

While the truth of (T) confirms to some extent the truth of (H), it does not prove (H) deductively. (T) fails to prove (H) with complete certainty because (T) might be implied and explained by some hypothesis other than (H). In this case, (T) could be true while (H) is false.

Neither is absolute proof produced in the case of disconfirmation (i.e., when the expected result does not occur). The procedure of disconfirmation can likewise be represented symbolically:

1. If (H) is true, then, assuming (A) is true, (T) will be true.
2. <u>(T) appears to be false.</u>
3. Therefore, (H) is probably false.

From the perspective of deductive logic, the above pattern of reasoning follows the rule known as *modus tollens*, according to which hypothesis (H) is conclusively disproved. In inductive reasoning, however, the falsity of (T) does not conclusively discredit (H), since (H) may be supported by other sorts of evidential tests or may be logically related to other hypotheses which are already confirmed. Hence, either independent evidential support or theoretical support may override the seemingly disconfirming case.

The third factor which makes induction probabilistic is that the additional assumptions may themselves be in error. Hence, the results of an empirical test—whether positive or negative—also reflect on the additional assumptions which were taken as true in order to check the given hypothesis. There is a variety of circumstances under which these assumptions could come up for question and test. So, again, the evidential appraisal of any hypothesis is at best probable.

Obviously, the final assessment of a hypothesis is a complicated task. There is no pat formula for just "reading off" the probability or acceptability of a hypothesis from the evidence. There are too many subtleties, such as additional assumptions and alternative ways of viewing the evidence, which take the whole process beyond any simple decision. Although the processes of confirmation and disconfirmation in science have received sustained attention by logicians, these same basic processes occur in many areas of intellectual endeavor. For present purposes, it is the pattern of disconfirmation which shapes the evidential argument from evil. Christian theism is treated as an explanatory scheme which purports to explain important facts of the human condition. When certain facts do not seem to be encompassed or implied by this theistic scheme, they function as a kind of negative evidence against it. Evil is perhaps the most impressive piece of negative evidence which can be used to argue that theism is improbable or implausible.

Variant Renditions of the Evidential Problem

There are three identifiable versions of the evidential argument from evil, each of which employs the strategy of disconfirmation. Interestingly, these three renditions of the evidential argument correspond exactly to the three renditions of the logical argument. The evidential arguments involve the same propositions as did the logical arguments:

(G) An omnipotent, omniscient, wholly good God exists;

(E₁) Evil exists;

(E₂) Large amounts, extreme kinds, and perplexing distributions of evil exist;

(E₃) Gratuitous or pointless evil exists.

Instead of analyzing the consistency of (G) and some (E)-like proposition, as do the logical arguments, the evidential arguments take the various (E)-like propositions to constitute evidence against (G), or to provide rational grounds for rejecting (G).

The distinct structure of the three evidential arguments from evil is readily seen in Figure 2. Each of these arguments finds representation in the scholarly literature. However, their significance and popularity seem almost to be the reverse of their logical counterparts. Whereas formulation I is the classic logical problem, formulation VI is the most interesting and important evidential problem.

Contrary to what discussions of the logical problem suggest, many traditional theodicists can be interpreted as being concerned primarily with the evidential problem. The arguments of, say, Augustine or Leibniz apply to the evidential argument from evil. Nevertheless, the logical and evidential problems are not as clearly distin-

Figure 2
Evidential Arguments from Evil

IV	V	VI
(G)	(G)	(G)
is improbable	is improbable	is improbable
on	on	on
(E₁)	(E₂)	(E₃)

guished in traditional writings as they are in contemporary studies. As the two types of argument began to be differentiated in the recent past, the logical problem seemed to preoccupy the minds of both critics and defenders of theism. Now, interest in the evidential problem is ostensibly rising, but there is no systematic response to it from the perspective of orthodox theism.

In the remainder of this section, brief attention will be given to formulations IV and V of the evidential argument; formulation VI will occupy us throughout the rest of the book.

Formulation IV of the evidential problem charges that the fact that

(E₁) Evil exists

counts against the claim that

(G) An omnipotent, omniscient, wholly good God exists.

One advocate of this approach is George Schlesinger, who treats theism as a kind of hypothesis amenable to evidential test and recognizes that evil in the world tends to disconfirm it: "It is not merely that the theistic hypothesis seems to lack positive support which would lead merely to agnosticism: there appears to be strong *prima facie* evidence that it is false and thus atheism seems supported."[10] Schlesinger thinks that questions about the kinds and multiplicity of actual evil are beside the point. The sheer existence of evil in the world is *prima facie* negative evidence. He explains: "In an attempt to shed more light on our topic let me stress that while the ques-

10. George Schlesinger, *Religion and Scientific Method* (Hingham, MA: Reidel, 1977), p. 13.

tion of the amount of evil the world contains most vitally affects our lives, in the context of our problem this is an entirely irrelevant question."[11] In terms of our notation, Schlesinger's point is that (E_1) constitutes evidence against the truth or acceptability of (G).

As might be expected, the proper reply to this evidential problem is parallel to that for the corresponding logical problem. Once it is recognized that the atheist must include some auxiliary assumptions in order to make theistic claims capable of empirical evaluation, it is relatively easy to locate the source of trouble. The atheist fallaciously uses additional propositions which the theist either does not or need not accept. In the present instance, the atheistic critic employs the dubious assumption that God would not allow the existence of any evil whatsoever. Although some critics of theism adopt this assumption, orthodox theists have never officially held such a belief. Neither is it a universal and necessary truth such that anyone who considers it must accept it. Thus, it is difficult to see how such an assumption can create a problem for theism proper.

A full theistic reply to formulation IV of the evidential problem vis-à-vis the God-allows-no-evil presumption could include proposals of morally sufficient reasons why God might allow at least some evil to exist (e.g., as a potential result of free will or the continual operation of nature), or could merely express the confidence that God must have some morally sufficient reason for allowing evil (since we already have some independent grounds for believing in His existence and goodness), though we may not know what this reason is. Without assessing the merit of these answers here, mentioning them still suffices to show that the bare fact of evil does not count heavily against Christian theism.

11. Ibid., p. 14.

Of course, another possible reply is simply to deny that evil exists, that is, to refuse to grant the evidential premise (E_1). While this option is attractive to some groups (e.g., Christian Science), it is hardly open to the orthodox Christian theist whose explicit position involves belief in the existence of evil. Moreover, such denials of evil stretch our ordinary moral judgments to the breaking point, and promise relief from the problem of evil at the high price of ethical agnosticism. Ultimately, denials of evil simply evade the problem rather than face it.

Although formulation IV is a legitimate evidential argument, its reliance upon the sheer existence of evil provides very weak evidence against theism. Perhaps it is not the fact of evil itself, but the great degree and profusion of evil, which creates a formidable problem for theistic commitment. In other words, it is (E_2) and not (E_1) which supplies the weightier negative evidence. Thus we are brought to a consideration of formulation V of the evidential problem.

Harvard theologian Gordon Kaufman discusses the force of this formulation of the problem of evil. In *God: The Problem*, Kaufman struggles to make the concept of God intelligible to contemporary man, but realizes that the concept seems falsified by the terrible facts of evil:

> A major stumbling block for contemporary faith in God remains: If there is a God, and if he is loving, why is there such horrendous evil in the world? Do not the facts of terror, pain, and unjustifiable suffering demonstrate either that God is not good—and therefore not worthy of our adoration and worship—or that there is no God at all? . . . Exploration of the *varieties, subtleties,* and *enormities* of evil in human life has become perhaps the principal theme of literature, art, and drama since World War II.[12]

12. Gordon D. Kaufman, *God: The Problem* (Cambridge, MA: Harvard University, 1972), pp. 171–72. (italics mine)

Kaufman is one of many authors who recognize that the fact that

(E$_2$) Large amounts, extreme kinds, and perplexing distributions of evil exist

generates a serious problem for Christian theism. This fact casts grave doubt on the central theistic belief that

(G) An omnipotent, omniscient, wholly good God exists.

In *The Faith of a Heretic* Walter Kaufmann is troubled by this same kind of problem:

> The problem arises when monotheism is enriched with— or impoverished by—two assumptions: that God is omnipotent and that God is just. In fact, popular theism goes beyond merely asserting that God is just and claims that God is "good," that he is morally perfect, that he hates suffering, that he loves man, and that he is infinitely merciful, far transcending all human mercy, love, and perfection. Once these assumptions are granted, the problem arises: why, then, is there *all* the suffering we know? And as long as these assumptions are granted, this question cannot be answered. For if these assumptions were true, it would follow that there could not be all this suffering. Conversely: since it is a fact that there is *all this* suffering, it is plain that at least one of these assumptions must be false. Popular theism is refuted by the existence of *so much* suffering. The theism preached from thousands of pulpits and credited by millions of believers is disproved by Auschwitz and *a billion* lesser evils.[13]

13. Walter Kaufmann, *The Faith of a Heretic* (Garden City, NY: Doubleday, 1961), p. 139. (italics mine)

Again, the point is that the evils we witness are so severe and widespread that the existence of God seems highly improbable.

Formulating a reply to the problem of the low probability of (G) given (E₂) is a difficult matter. However, adequate reply is not impossible and can proceed in somewhat the same manner as our response to formulation IV. Essentially, the troublesome assumption in the atheistic attack now is that a loving and just God would allow only a certain amount of evil and no more. But this is hard to justify. In principle, how much evil is *too much* for God to allow? Furthermore, how could we ever ascertain that the present amount of evil in the world far exceeds the divinely set limit? These and other perplexing questions make it difficult to imagine how the atheist could ever establish such claims. There does not seem to be any clear limit placed upon evil by Christian theology. Neither is there any accepted method by which one could ascertain whether such a limit has been surpassed.

Perhaps there is a sense, however, in which this formulation of the evidential argument has a point. At least this evidential argument forcefully discounts any claim for a deity who places a felicitous limitation on the evils which human beings can experience. Thus, the god of popular, easy theism really is dead. The burden then falls upon the shoulders of thinking Christian theists to articulate a concept of God which is more sophisticated and profound than popular theism envisions.

This route of rebuttal seems much more promising than the route of denying that there really is as much evil, or that multitudes of people are really as unhappy, as is initially supposed. It is better simply to admit that there is a great deal of evil and suffering in the world, and then to argue that the existence of God is neither precluded nor made unlikely thereby. Although such a rebuttal must be fleshed out in more detail, that need not be done here. The next rendition of the evidential problem, formulation VI, rests upon an even stronger factual claim: that many evils in the world are not only severe and unbearable but are utterly gratuitous. The theistic reply to formulation VI applies, with appropriate adaptation, to formulation V as well.

The Argument from Gratuitous Evil

The argument from gratuitous evil presents the most serious formulation of the evidential problem of evil. In fact, it may well be the most formidable of all statements of the problem of evil. Of course, no evidential argument from evil can be called "strong" in the sense that its inherent structure is logically tighter than that of the logical arguments from evil. In this sense, the various logical arguments are obviously stronger. However, in the sense that the evidential problems pose challenges which are more difficult for the theist to rebut, they are more serious or more formidable than their logical counterparts. It is in this sense that the evidential arguments are stronger, and the argument from gratuitous evil is the most forceful of these.

Formulation VI represents the problem of whether the fact, or at least the alleged fact, that

(E_3) Gratuitous or pointless evil exists

constitutes significant evidence against the belief that

(G) An omnipotent, omniscient, wholly good God exists.

James W. Cornman and Keith Lehrer propose that Christian theism is defeated by the evidence of (E_3). In *Philo-*

sophical Problems and Arguments, they present their case from evil in the guise of a provocative thought experiment:

> If you were all-good, all-knowing, and all-powerful and you were going to create a universe in which there were sentient beings—beings that are happy and sad; enjoy pleasure, feel pain; express love, anger, pity, hatred—what kind of world would you create? . . . Try to imagine what such a world would be like. Would it be like the one which actually does exist, this world we live in? Would you create a world such as this one if you had the power and know-how to create any logically possible world? If your answer is "no," as it seems to be, then you should begin to understand why the evil of suffering and pain in this world is such a problem for anyone who thinks God created this world. . . . Given this world, then, it seems, we should conclude that it is *improbable* that it was created or sustained by anything we would call God. Thus, given this particular world, it seems that we should conclude that it is *improbable* that God—who, if he exists, created the world—exists. Consequently, the belief that God does not exist, rather than the belief that he exists, would seem to be *justified by the evidence* we find in this world.[14]

After making clear that their inductive case is based on the sheer evidence of evil, which in and of itself reduces the probability of theism, Cornman and Lehrer emphasize that the most devastating evidence is constituted by fortuitous or unnecessary evil:

> At this stage of the discussion we seem warranted in concluding that the existence of what surely seems to be *unnecessary evil* in this world provides *inductive grounds*

14. James W. Cornman and Keith Lehrer, *Philosophical Problems and Arguments: An Introduction* (New York: Macmillan, 1970), pp. 340–41. (italics mine)

for the belief that God does not exist, because it is *probable* that if he once existed he would have created a different world and that if he now exists he would control the course of nature so as to avoid many pernicious events that occur.[15]

An increasing number of powerful expressions of the problem of gratuitous evil can be found in the scholarly literature. William Rowe also provides a very clear statement of the argument:

We must then ask whether it is *reasonable* to believe that all the instances of profound, *seemingly pointless human and animal suffering* lead to greater goods. And, if they should somehow all lead to greater goods, is it *reasonable* to believe that an omnipotent, omniscient being could not have brought about *any* of those goods without permitting the instances of suffering which supposedly lead to them? When we consider these more general questions in the light of our experience and knowledge of the variety and profusion of human and animal suffering occurring daily in our world, it seems that *the answer must be no*. It seems *quite unlikely* that all the instances of intense human and animal suffering occurring daily in our world lead to greater goods, and *even more unlikely* that if they all do, an omnipotent, omniscient being could not have achieved at least some of those goods without permitting the instances of suffering that lead to them. In the light of our experience and knowledge of the variety and scale of human and animal suffering in our world, the idea that none of these instances of suffering could have been prevented by an omnipotent being without the loss of a greater good seems an *extraordinary, absurd idea, quite beyond our belief.*[16]

15. Ibid., p. 347. (italics mine)
16. Rowe, *Philosophy*, p. 89. (italics mine)

Similar statements of the problem of gratuitous evil could be multiplied indefinitely, but the preceding ones sufficiently express the issue.

These relatively technical statements of the problem of gratuitous evil display a refined manner of expressing a very common and widespread hesitation about Christian belief. Although ordinary persons cannot always articulate precisely why apparently meaningless evils tend to destroy their belief in God, their thoughts can often be arranged into the theoretical structure of the evidential argument from gratuitous evil. For the layman as well as the scholar, then, a persistent and pressing question is whether pointless evils render Christianity unbelievable or improbable.

Since the essential argument from gratuitous evil is often embedded within complex and lengthy philosophical discourse, it is helpful to present a simplified model of it. The model conforms to the general pattern of evidential reasoning already discussed. The position in question is, of course, the theistic claim that

(G) An omnipotent, omniscient, wholly good God exists.

In evaluating this claim, at least one auxiliary assumption is made. Many writers on the problem of gratuitous evil believe that God is utterly fastidious in preventing all evils from being gratuitous. This assumption may be labeled the principle of meticulous providence, and may be expressed thus:

(MP) An omnipotent, omniscient, wholly good God would prevent or eliminate the existence of really gratuitous or pointless evils.

This principle, together with (G), implies that the proposition

(E_3) Gratuitous or pointless evil exists

is false; that is, ($\sim E_3$) is true. But in fact (E_3) appears to be true. This is the heart of the problem.

The evidential argument from gratuitous evil can be condensed into the following model:

1. If (G) is true, then, assuming that (MP) is true, ($\sim E_3$) should be true.   (theological premise)
2. <u>It is probable that (E_3) is true.   (factual premise)</u>
3. Therefore, it is probable that (G) is false.   (logical conclusion)

No easy answers to this atheistic argument are readily available. The way in which the argument is constructed shows that the existence of what surely seems to be gratuitous evil counts against the existence of God. Each possible route of rebuttal involves complicated theoretical maneuvers by the theist.

The problem of gratuitous evil has emerged here as the most formidable of all the evidential arguments against theism. Since its logic is inductively correct, a response depends on the rejection of at least one of its premises. Attempts to refute the premises lead to some very interesting and important insights about the nature of God and His disposition of good and evil.

4

Analyzing the Argument from Gratuitous Evil

A New Challenge from Evil

In recent years, philosophers have witnessed the demise of the logical version of the problem of evil.[1] Yet there is a growing opinion that evil constitutes a somewhat different kind of challenge to Christian theism, namely, that evil—even if it cannot be used to deduce an inconsistency within theism—provides strong evidence against theistic belief. No response to the problem of evil is complete unless it addresses this increasingly important line of argument. Chapter 3 identified the most crucial formulation of the evidential argument as that which is based on apparently gratuitous evil. In the present chapter, the elements of this formulation will be analyzed in detail. In the next chapter, a rebuttal of the argument will be attempted.

The central theistic claim in question is:

> (G) An omnipotent, omniscient, wholly good God exists.

1. This demise has largely been due to the efforts of Alvin Plantinga, Keith Yandell, John Hick, M. B. Ahern, and several others who have provided serious rebuttals from a theistic point of view.

What may be called the evidential argument from gratuitous evil takes the following proposition as significant evidence against (G):

(E_3) Gratuitous or pointless evil exists.

According to many authors, (E_3) makes (G) improbable, implausible, or unlikely. Some philosophers who advance this argument have tried to specify in precise quantitative terms the low degree of probability which (E_3) confers upon (G), but their efforts have been short-lived.[2] Nevertheless, there is a genuine sense in which (E_3) can be taken to reduce the rational acceptability of (G). The sense of probability involved here is used in rational discussion generally.

Statements of the evidential argument from gratuitous evil are not difficult to find in the contemporary literature. We have already cited a statement of the argument by James W. Cornman and Keith Lehrer and another by William Rowe (pp. 74–75). But perhaps the clearest and most succinct statement of the argument is provided by Edward Madden and Peter Hare in *Evil and the Concept of God:*

> If God is unlimited in power and goodness, why is there so much *prima facie* gratuitous evil in the world? If he is unlimited in power he should be able to remove unnecessary evil, and if he is unlimited in goodness, he would want to remove it, but he does not. Apparently he is limited either in power or goodness, or does not exist at all.[3]

2. See Wesley Salmon, "Religion and Science: A New Look at Hume's *Dialogues,*" *Philosophical Studies* 33 (1978): 143–76; Nancy Cartwright, "Comments on Wesley Salmon's 'Science and Religion,' " *Philosophical Studies* 33 (1978): 177–83; and Alvin Plantinga, "The Probabilistic Argument from Evil," *Philosophical Studies* 35 (1979): 1–53.

3. Edward Madden and Peter Hare, *Evil and the Concept of God* (Springfield, IL: Charles C. Thomas, 1968), p. 3.

Essentially, Madden and Hare take the *prima facie* truth of (E_3) to count as evidence against (G).

What must be recognized, however, is that the disconfirming effect of (E_3) is mediated by the assumption that God would allow no genuinely gratuitous evil. In chapter 3 this assumption was labeled the principle of meticulous providence and stated explicitly as follows:

> (MP) An omnipotent, omniscient, wholly good God would prevent or eliminate the existence of really gratuitous or pointless evils.

It is important to note that at this point no reason need be given why God would not allow really gratuitous evils. There are numerous reasons offered in the literature. All that matters here is that this principle is widely held. It is also helpful to remember that no complete definition of "evil" or even of "gratuitous evil" need be given for the basic argument to stand. Virtually any definition of "gratuitous evil" could simply be substituted into the original context of debate and then the argument could proceed as before.

At this point we should review our symbolic model of the argument from gratuitous evil (p. 77):

1. If (G) is true, then, assuming that (MP) is true, ($\sim E_3$) should be true.   (theological premise)
2. It is probable that (E_3) is true.   (factual premise)
3. Therefore, it is probable that (G) is false.   (logical conclusion)

An argument may be criticized either in terms of its form (structure) or in terms of its content (premises). We have already characterized the structure of this argument as broadly inductive. We should not forget that inductive arguments by their very nature are nondemonstrative. In other words, such arguments do not provide absolute proof or disproof; they are not logically conclusive. This does not mean that we can give a proper theistic rebuttal simply by pointing out the inherent inconclusiveness of inductive reasoning. The very point of inductive reasoning is not to provide conclusiveness, but to supply a measure of probability or plausibility for the given conclusion.[4] However, recognizing the inconclusiveness of inductive argumentation does mean that evil—even gratuitous evil—is not the last word in the assessment of theism. Evil is *prima facie* evidence to be sure; but there are other considerations, rational and experiential as well as evidential, which also affect the final verdict. In fact, many of these other arguments strongly support theism. Nevertheless, there are serious thinkers who regard the argument from gratuitous evil as so impressive that it outweighs all other arguments. Indeed, they believe that the problem of gratuitous evil supplies sufficient rational grounds for rejecting Christian theism.

The task at hand is to examine carefully the two basic premises in the argument. If just one of these two premises can be rebutted, the atheistic conclusion can be avoided. It will soon become apparent that an attempt to rebut either of the two impinges upon a number of complex philosophical issues.

The Factual Premise of the Argument

The factual claim about the existence of gratuitous evil is expressed in a variety of ways, all of which display the *a posteriori* nature of the proposition. Terms such as

4. See Edward Madden and Peter Hare, "Evil and Inconclusiveness," *Sophia* 11 (1972): 12. The point is simply that a kind of inconclusiveness is characteristic of evidential or inductive reasoning.

"probable," "plausible," and "likely" are frequently employed to qualify the claim. For present purposes, such qualifiers come to roughly the same point: given the way certain evils appear to us, it is reasonable to believe that they have no point or purpose. Regardless of how this claim is expressed, it is common for philosophers entering the debate to view it as the premise which will make or break the overall argument from gratuitous evil.

Theists and atheists alike frequently assume that the principle of meticulous providence is clearly true and thus agree that the factual claim, that there probably is gratuitous evil, is the crucial point of contention. Madden and Hare state that "the really interesting problem of evil is whether the apparent gratuity can be explained away by more ingenious measures or whether the gratuity is real and hence detrimental to religious belief."[5] William Rowe, who argues for an atheistic conclusion to the debate, writes: "If we are to fault this argument, . . . we must find some fault with its [factual] premise."[6] Keith Yandell, a theist, insists that "the crucial question is whether it is certain, or at least more probable than not, that there is unjustified evil, whether natural or moral. . . ."[7] A list of similar statements could be continued indefinitely. Given this intense interest, we must carefully examine the claim that

(E_3) Pointless or gratuitous evil exists.

The debate over this premise is more complex than might first be expected.

5. Madden and Hare, *Evil and the Concept of God*, p. 3.
6. William Rowe, *Philosophy of Religion: An Introduction* (Belmont, CA: Dickenson, 1978), p. 88.
7. Keith Yandell, *Basic Issues in the Philosophy of Religion* (Boston: Allyn and Bacon, 1971), pp. 62–63.

Debate over the Factual Premise

One helpful way of understanding the status of the factual premise is to pose the question of what atheistic philosophers would have to do to substantiate it, and the question of what theistic philosophers would have to do to refute it.

The atheist who advances the evidential problem of gratuitous evil must rationally support his contention that there is, or probably is, gratuitous evil. The overall strategy involved here becomes quite complicated, yet one key move is identifiable. The atheist must argue that many instances of evil cannot be justified on either *extrinsic* grounds (e.g., the promotion of greater goods, the prevention of greater evils, etc.) or *intrinsic* grounds (e.g., conformity to some ideal standard of goodness or meaning), and thus are gratuitous. It is not uncommon for atheistic writers to support the belief in gratuitous evil by describing some very significant evils in ways which accent their seemingly gratuitous character, or by cataloguing an impressive number of evils which appear to be gratuitous. But exactly what does this approach to the factual premise accomplish or fail to accomplish?

To take these two questions in reverse order, this approach fails to prove that there are no extrinsic or intrinsic grounds upon which the evils in question are meaningful or justified (i.e., not gratuitous). All it really shows is that there do not seem to be any such grounds, that we do not know what they could be, or at least that the person drawing the atheistic conclusion does not know what they could be. But to know this claim with certainty would require omniscience or an Archimedean vantage point on the world. After all, we are familiar with cases in which our first interpretation of the facts turned out not to be correct at all. In the present debate, theodicists have been fairly persuasive in pointing out that some apparently meaningless evils are not really meaningless (e.g., suffering can build character). Hence, theodicists correctly remind us of the tentative and fallible nature of the assertion that there is genuinely gratuitous evil.

What the atheistic approach to the factual premise does show is that, as long as the theist is committed to the principle that God would not allow really gratuitous evil, there appears to be counterevidence to theistic commitment. There is a *prima facie* conflict between what theism holds about the world and the way the world actually seems to be. Although the theist might offer plausible explanations why many apparently gratuitous evils are not really gratuitous, the atheistic opponent has at least succeeded in showing that theism encounters initial difficulty. The theist must come to grips with the facts which tend to falsify his claims about God. The evidential problem of gratuitous evil, therefore, is not a contrived or foreign consideration, but a problem which the theist has created for himself. His own conceptual commitments generate it and his further explanations must resolve it.

What, then, shall we say about the status of the factual premise? Shall we believe that there is gratuitous evil or that there is not? Or that there probably is or probably is not? Let us quickly review the issue step by step. Theists typically state or imply that God allows no gratuitous evil. Atheists indicate that gratuitous evil does seem to exist. Theists respond by giving reasons, or, in full form, theodicies, why apparently gratuitous evil can be interpreted instead as meaningful.

Of course, the continuing debate regarding the truth or probable truth of the factual claim requires further thrusts and parries. The atheist must show that major theodicies fail to account for some significant evils in the world. Furthermore, he must argue that there is no good reason to expect that new theodicies or permutations of old ones will ever be successful. If the atheist can do this, he will thereby have shown that it is more reasonable to believe that the factual premise is true than to believe it is false. In short, he will have cited rational grounds for believing that there are gratuitous evils.

Now the theist, on the other side, must continue to strengthen existing theodicies which seem correct and helpful. Moreover, he must construct a good argument to the effect that all evils are in principle covered by the theodicies offered, although there is no reason for his having to show in detail just how each individual evil is covered. If the theist can do all this, he will have gone a long way toward showing that it is more reasonable to believe that the factual premise is false than to believe it true. He will thereby have supplied rational grounds for believing that there is in fact no gratuitous evil.

Both of these respective strategies seem correct so far. But in looking at the contemporary state of the debate, it is apparent that neither the atheist nor the theist has succeeded. One weakness which frequently occurs in atheistic attempts to prove the factual premise is the unexamined assumption that the successive addition of instances of apparently gratuitous evil increases the likelihood that there *is* gratuitous evil. But whether there really is gratuitous evil must be argued on the basis of each particular instance or on the basis of some defensible general theory. From the sheer fact that there are many instances of apparently gratuitous evil, one must not hastily conclude that any instance or that all instances are really gratuitous. This not only begs the question entirely, but also increases the temptation to argue on a strictly emotional basis.

Theistic efforts, too, are not without shortcomings. One flaw in many theodicies is that they tacitly assume that God exists and then argue against gratuitous evil with this confidence smuggled in. But within the framework of the problem of evil, this is an illicit assumption, since

God's existence is the very thing in question. For example, Gottfried Leibniz in his *Theodicy* took God's existence as a given for his discussion of evil. From that point, Leibniz simply argued that, since God would undoubtedly create the best of all possible worlds, the created world must indeed be the best possible one. Whenever the theist makes this kind of mistake, the question of whether there is real gratuitous evil is begged, not argued.

Obviously, if the theist has convincing independent grounds for believing in God's existence (whether rational, historical, or experiential), these will have a bearing on his assessment of evils in the world. Now in light of the possibility of such independent arguments, how must the problem of evil be treated? Clearly, these arguments would have to be included in any complete evaluation of the theistic world-view. But in that overall evaluation each of the theistic arguments must be assessed on its own merits, an enterprise of no small proportions. Can talk of evil be suspended until the outcome of some of these other issues is known? Not very easily. And if the atheist likewise claims that he has reasons for the rejection of theism which are completely independent of the problem of evil, the issue becomes further complicated.

What is needed, therefore, is to find out how much can be determined about gratuitous evil within the context of the problem itself, without drawing from allegedly independent arguments. Besides, it is not at all clear what definitive conclusion regarding God's existence could be reached in these other areas apart from the crucial consideration of evil. The problem of evil is certainly a key issue, and, for some, *the* key issue, in the complex question of the validity of Christian theism.

If we take a sort of purist position on the problem of evil, then we will want to hold in abeyance other argu-

ments for and against God's existence, and thereby hope
to rid the debate of some common theistic and atheistic
fallacies. Recognizing the failures of both sides, as well as
their partial successes, we might conclude that the debate
over the existence of gratuitous evil is deadlocked and
thus adopt a position of agnosticism on the question. Since
the atheist's attempt to establish the premise that there
is (or surely appears to be) gratuitous evil and the theist's
attempt to rebut it may seem equally strong (or weak),
we may think that it is most rational to suspend belief on
the matter.

We should understand well, however, the impact of such
an agnostic stance on the question of gratuitous evil. If an
agnostic judgment on the issue of gratuitous evil results,
it actually works to the advantage of the atheist. The atheist need not prove beyond a shadow of a doubt that there
is gratuitous evil, but only that there are cases of apparently gratuitous evil which the theist cannot readily explain within his own system. Again, the point is that the
evidential problem of evil is essentially the theist's problem: the theist holds a position typically taken to imply
that there should be no gratuitous evil and yet there appear to be some gratuitous evils. Hence, the burden of
proof is on the theist to remove the discrepancy. The atheist can simply urge that his case from gratuitous evil,
regardless of whether it demonstrates conclusively that
gratuitous evil exists, still shows that the difficulty is of
such magnitude that theism ought not be affirmed.[8] In
the last analysis, then, atheistic efforts to show that there
is or probably is gratuitous evil serve to emphasize the
serious problem facing the theist and thus supply a good
reason for not believing that theism is true.

8. A kind of rational stalemate is all that the atheist needs to obtain when
employing the evidential problem of gratuitous evil.

How to View the Factual Premise

As long as the theist understands his theological position to entail that there are no gratuitous evils, and as long as his efforts to show that there are none fall markedly shy of complete success, his conceptual commitments will always be in tension with ordinary experience of evil in the world. Theism will be forever plagued by a systematically insoluble problem. This is why a shift in much theistic thinking about gratuitous evil may be advisable, a shift which is faithful to the essential commitments of theism *and* solves the problem of gratuitous evil. Were the theist to admit both the possibility and actuality of some gratuitous evil, he still has a viable direction to take. In terms of the present argument from gratuitous evil, the theist could grant the factual premise, which has traditionally been the main point of contention. Then the way to prevent the atheistic argument from going through is to refuse to grant its other premise, which involves the principle that God allows no gratuitous evil. If the principle of meticulous providence is extricated from the interpretation of theistic commitment, then the theological premise of the argument does not hold. And if this premise does not hold, the argument cannot succeed.

Relinquishing the theological premise is not simply an *ad hoc* maneuver designed to provide immediate relief from a critical problem. It offers at least two important benefits to the theist who wrestles with the problem of evil. First, accepting the existence of some gratuitous evil is more consonant with our common experience than is the position which denies gratuitous evil *a priori*. Second, rejecting the principle of meticulous providence opens the way for a deeper and more profound apprehension of God than that widely accepted principle allows. This shift makes possible a theodicy for our day which is both experientially and conceptually adequate. To begin the development of this theodicy, a case for the acceptance of the premise that there is or probably is gratuitous evil must be made. (Why the principle of meticulous providence should be rejected will be discussed in the closing sections of this chapter and in the next chapter.)

The efforts of both theists and atheists who debate the existence of gratuitous evil must be accorded great respect. The enterprise of philosophical theology is richer for their contributions. However, it should not be automatically presumed that their efforts have approximately the same weight and that final judgment on the point must be diplomatically suspended. Although both sides have constructed strong and important arguments, one particular argument tips the scales in favor of the premise that there exists gratuitous evil, an argument on which atheists themselves often fail to capitalize. This argument, simply put, insists on a general faithfulness to the common human experience of evil in the world. Since human experience registers the existence of some evils as being utterly gratuitous, it is more reasonable simply to accept the factual premise that gratuitous evil exists.

There is little doubt that a person's experience is conditioned by a multitude of factors: beliefs, attitudes, and even neural and chemical states. Since these factors differ among individuals, we cannot be too dogmatic in making pronouncements about what persons do or should experience. Yet, for the most part, philosophers have been successful in locating common elements in human experience, whether in the perception of simple material properties, such as colors, or the awareness of more highly abstract and interpretive phenomena, such as time. While these and other elements in human experience may sometimes be mistaken or distorted, they are generally reliable. In fact, it is the overall reliability of experience which serves to detect and correct its own errors. We cannot imagine what it would be for human experience, on whatever level of complexity, to be inherently unreliable. So many ingredients of human life and knowledge come to us through the avenues of experience that to deny its general validity is to raise the radical question of whether we are capable of knowing anything at all. This is why the position of strong skepticism has never gained consistent acceptance by anyone.

All of this has an interesting relationship to the debate over whether there is in fact gratuitous evil. It is common for both theist and atheist to agree that many of the evils of our world initially *appear* to be gratuitous; this seems to be part of our common human experience. The atheist seeks to establish the gratuitous character of these evils by further argument, and the theist typically seeks to argue that such evils are not *really* gratuitous. Clearly, theists have sometimes been successful in discovering the meaning or justification of certain apparently gratuitous evils or kinds of evils. Thus, theists have succeeded in correcting or adjusting some of our initial experiences of evil, and this kind of occasional correction is normal. But to think that theists have shown (or could show) all *prima facie* gratuitous evils to be meaningful and justified is to adopt unwittingly a kind of skepticism regarding our experience of value and disvalue in the world. This is a higher price than any of us should be willing to pay.

The insistence that we not unduly discredit our common human experience of evil can be given both philosophical and theological force. Philosophically speaking, we should be wary about dismissing the more obvious in favor of the less obvious. In the present context, this implies that the persistent human experience of gratuitous evil comes with better credentials than the *a priori* denial of any gratuitous evil in a theistic universe. If the theist discredits this important aspect of human experience, it is difficult to see how he can confidently proceed to discuss the problem at hand (not to mention other important issues which also have basis in experience). A theistic case against gratuitous evil casts grave doubt on the reliability of human experience and on the moral and rational categories which condition it, and thus runs the risk of being self-defeating.

Theologically speaking, it is not clear that the theist himself would want to be saddled with the consequences of such a position. The belief that God created man with generally trustworthy rational and moral faculties is a standard component of almost all versions of Christian theism. Hence, it may be unwittingly inconsistent for the theist to claim that the human experience of gratuitous evil is regularly and systematically mistaken. This is not to suggest that all of our immediate or snap judgments about such things have some kind of divine guarantee. Not everything is really as it appears, and some apparently meaningless evils are found to be meaningful after careful investigation. Nevertheless, when the weight of human experience—both personal and historical—still registers many evils as pointless, extreme caution must be exercised in suggesting that such experience is spurious. Indeed, if the human experience of gratuitous evil were unfailingly wrong, the very fact that it is unfailingly wrong would surely have no good theological explanation, and would be a strong candidate for a gratuitous evil itself.

The attempt of theodicists to deny that there is gratuitous evil, then, is not experientially based. Such attempts are motivated by the preconception that God does not allow gratuitous evil, the principle of meticulous providence. As long as the theist understands his theological position to include this principle, he will have to reinterpret a significant part of human experience. The resultant tension between the actual experience of the world, on the one hand, and what theism presumably says that experience should be, on the other hand, is very great.

Much of the history of theodicy can be organized around

those who choose to retain one pole of the tension and reject the other. Traditional theodicists characteristically maintain that there is no gratuitous evil and thus override the evidence of experience. Since this traditional orientation stems from the very logic of the concepts contained in a theistic view, it may be called a *conceptual* mode of doing theodicy. Modern theodicists tend to favor the construction of a theistic system on the basis of broad features of human experience. Hence, they opt for an *experiential* mode of theodicy. However, thinkers on both sides commit certain errors. Traditional theodicy preserves conceptual commitments but fails to take sufficient account of experience.[9] Modern theodicy promises to take sufficient account of experience but modifies certain conceptual elements of theism to do so.[10] What is needed is a theodicy which avoids both of these weaknesses and unites the conceptual and experiential elements.

The only way to remain faithful to the experience of gratuitous evil and at the same time retain a properly theistic conception of the world is to admit the fact that there is gratuitous evil, and to eliminate the curious theological principle which requires that there is no gratuitous evil. This entails the rejection of the theological premise in the evidential argument from gratuitous evil, and paves the way for a defense of theism which is both experientially and conceptually adequate.

The Principle of Meticulous Providence

Now that the existence of genuinely gratuitous evils as a truth of experience has been admitted, the way to de-

9. I.e., traditional theodicy retains the principle of meticulous providence and reinterprets the experience of gratuitous evil to conform to it. Augustine, Aquinas, Leibniz, and others take this course.

10. I.e., modern theodicy preserves the experience of gratuitous evil and then alters one or more of the divine attributes in order to account for it. Edgar Brightman, Karl Barth, Alfred North Whitehead, and others take this course.

fend against the evidential argument is to show why there is a place for some gratuitous evil within a theistic conception of the world. Such a defense involves qualifying theism so that *prima facie* gratuitous evils, and even really gratuitous evils, do not count as evidence against it. Such a qualification is not a contrived evasion of the facts of evil. Instead it involves a sophisticated explanation of theism which allows gratuitous evil, and thereby changes the evidential import of the facts of evil. If the theist can locate a place for gratuitous evil in his system, then the original theological premise does not hold. Hence the atheistic argument from gratuitous evil fails.

Consider the essential argument as contained in our model:

1. If (G) is true, then, assuming that (MP) is true, (∼E₃) should be true.   (theological premise)
2. It is probable that (E₃) is true.   (factual premise)
3. Therefore, it is probable that (G) is false.   (logical conclusion)

Obviously, this argument is effectively rebutted if either one of its premises can be shown false or unacceptable. It seems best not to exhaust our energies trying to disprove premise 2, which involves the factual claim that

(E₃) Gratuitous or pointless evil exists.

Instead, we should closely examine and eventually reject premise 1. This premise, as we have seen, incorporates the very widespread, but not incontestable, assumption that

(MP) An omnipotent, omniscient, wholly good God would prevent or eliminate the existence of really gratuitous or pointless evils.

This is the principle of meticulous providence, a principle which is commonly believed to express a necessary implication of the proposition that

> (G) An omnipotent, omniscient, wholly good God exists.

(G) is the fundamental theistic position in question. Insofar as (MP) is viewed as crucially linked to (G), (G) tends to be disconfirmed by (E_3).

Both sides of the debate characteristically assume that (MP), or some version of it, is entirely sound. It is supposed to be a proposition which is either a necessary truth (say of logic or ethics) or an essential component of orthodox Christian theology, and thus a belief which the theist *must* retain. Various authors have tried to urge this point. In support of a premise which corresponds closely to (MP), William Rowe writes that it "seems to express a belief that accords with our basic moral principles, principles shared by both theists and nontheists."[11] In discussing a principle much like (MP), Terence Penelhum claims that the denial of genuinely gratuitous evil is integral to theism: "It is logically inconsistent for a theist to admit the existence of a pointless evil."[12]

Conceptions of Gratuitous Evil

There is much agreement that God allows no gratuitous evil, and this consensus is expressed in the principle of meticulous providence. However, authors sometimes have

11. Rowe, *Philosophy*, p. 88.
12. Terence Penelhum, "Divine Goodness and the Problem of Evil," in *Readings in the Philosophy of Religion: An Analytic Approach*, ed. Baruch Brody (Englewood Cliffs, NJ: Prentice-Hall, 1974), p. 226.

different grounds for holding (MP). Interestingly enough, (MP) seems to follow from various ethical or theological orientations. Although (MP) is formulated here in a way which transcends these differing orientations, a brief exploration of them will shed light on why (MP) has been accepted. There seem to be two basic ethico-theological frameworks which can be taken as supporting (MP): one is teleological in character and the other is deontological. The former position evaluates an evil on the basis of extrinsic considerations; the latter evaluates an evil in terms of its intrinsic nature.

In the current literature on God and evil, the teleological approach is the more common one. In fact, theists and atheists frequently use teleological criteria in discussing the issue of gratuitous evil: evils are appraised with reference to their relations to other goods and evils. An evil is *justified* if, and only if, it is necessary to the existence of some actual or possible greater good, or to the prevention or elimination of some greater evil; an evil is *gratuitous* if it bears no such relations. Authors who deny that there is gratuitous evil in this sense typically articulate the denial in one of the following ways: that God sees to it that every individual evil is outweighed by some good, that He insures that this world contains on balance more good than evil, that He created the best of all possible worlds, or the like. As Keith Yandell writes: "The orthodox theist is committed to the truth of some version of the greater good defense."[13] Whether Yandell's point is correct will be discussed in the next chapter. It suffices here to emphasize the long-standing tendency to understand theism in this way.

The deontological orientation is more difficult to define than is the teleological. Yet, if given adequate formulation, the deontological orientation is the stronger one and hence

13. Keith Yandell, "The Greater Good Defense," *Sophia* 13 (1974): 1.

gives rise to a more serious problem. In the deontological view, an evil is regarded as *justified* or *gratuitous* on the basis of some internal property which it possesses, or fails to possess, or on the basis of its conformity, or lack of it, to some absolute standard of goodness or meaning. Thus, authors who share this perspective scrutinize evils according to whether they are somehow meaningful in themselves, and not on the basis of their consequences. This fundamental approach is echoed in the saying that no one, not even God, may do evil that good may come.

Dostoevsky's Ivan made this kind of point with Alyosha when he urged that no higher harmony could justify or make meaningful the suffering of just one poor child.[14] Madden and Hare seem to sponsor the same sort of view, as they often argue against theism by attempting to show not merely that there are horrendous evils which do not promote future goods, but that no future goods could justify or compensate for those evils anyway.[15] Whatever terms these and other authors use—"genuinely gratuitous evil," "absolute evil," "ultimately meaningless evil," "surd evil," or the like—they are convinced that the God of Christian theism cannot allow such evil to exist within His creation.

There is no point here in trying to reach a definitive statement regarding which of the two ethico-theological orientations provides the proper undergirding for the

14. Fyodor Dostoevsky, *The Brothers Karamazov*, trans. Constance Garnett (New York: Norton, 1976), pp. 222–27, especially p. 226.

15. Madden and Hare, *Evil and the Concept of God*, especially pp. 63–65. Other authors who discuss this matter of whether goods can somehow justify evils include: Arthur Schopenhauer, "On the Vanity and Suffering of Life," in the Supplements to the Fourth Book of *The World as Will and Idea*, trans. R. B. Haldane and J. Kemp (New York: AMS Press, 1976); George E. Moore, *Principia Ethica* (New York: Cambridge University, 1966), p. 30; Roderick Chisholm, "The Defeat of Good and Evil," *Proceedings of the American Philosophical Association* 42 (1968–1969): 21–38; David Ray Griffin, *God, Power, and Evil: A Process Theodicy* (Philadelphia: Westminster, 1976), pp. 21–22.

principle of meticulous providence. Both perspectives are important components of ethical and theological thinking;[16] and when the principle of meticulous providence is linked with either of these perspectives, serious problems regarding the concept of gratuitous evil result. Since Christian thinkers generally adopt the principle in question, they typically answer these problems on their own terms. They supply either teleological or deontological justifications for apparently gratuitous evils. If theists were to see that they need not accept the principle of meticulous providence, they would be able to answer the problems of gratuitous evil in entirely new ways. Our subsequent rebuttal of the principle is designed to hold regardless of whether it is rooted in a teleological or a deontological orientation.

If we grant the factual claim that there is gratuitous evil, the way to rebut the evidential argument from gratuitous evil is to find fault with its theological premise. Since the orthodox theism represented in the theological premise is not negotiable, the premise must instead be attacked by questioning the principle of meticulous providence which it involves. Although the principle may be thought to derive from some fundamental ethical and theological ideals, it can be shown to be unnecessary either to morality or to theism. Indeed a case can be made that the principle of meticulous providence conflicts with our best ethical and theological understanding. The next chapter selects two of the most important reasons why the principle must be rejected. One reason rests on the idea of a free moral order; the other stems from the idea

16. The teleological orientation is found in ethical theories such as utilitarianism, and in religious positions which affirm the purposes of God working through all things. The deontological orientation is found in ethical positions such as intuitionism and natural-law theory, and in positions which demand that we "must do justice though the heavens fall."

of a natural order. Once these ideas are delineated, a conception of the kind of world which embodies them can be developed. We will discover that some gratuitous evil is at least possible in such a world.

5

Toward a Theodicy for Our Day

The Need for Theodicy

In the 1960s Robert Coles, a research psychiatrist at the Harvard University Health Services, made a clinical study of the effects of racial discrimination in the South. One of the most fruitful methods of studying the perceptions of Southern children was to have them draw pictures of themselves and relevant features of their lives. Coles found that black children frequently distorted themselves and others of their race, clearly revealing their negative ideas about the human condition. Coles was particularly struck by the self-portrait of one little girl in Mississippi. After she had drawn the picture, the little girl's poignant response was: "That's me, and the Lord made me, but I must always remember that He did it, and it's His idea. So when I draw the Lord He'll be a real big man. He has to be to explain about the way things are."[1]

The little girl was not far wrong in thinking that God has to be a "real big man" in order to explain the way things are—not only in respect to racial problems, but the myriad evils which beset the human race. Discovering

1. Robert Coles, "When I Draw the Lord, He'll Be a Real Big Man," *The Atlantic Monthly* 217 (1966): 75.

101

the purposes of God in allowing evil has been the object of both popular dialogue and scholarly debate. Much of the problem is that God does not explicitly tell us why evil exists in great abundance. Instead we have been left with the task of figuring out God's reasons. As Harold DeWolf contends, "The greatest theoretical difficulty confronting the Christian faith is the problem of evil."[2] The goal of Christian theodicy, then, is to provide insight into the reasons for evil in a theistic universe.

Christian thinkers have not been without defense against the intellectual challenge posed by evil. Our understanding of God's ways is richer because they have labored to find a solution to this enigma. Those who study the broad sweep of Christian theodicy will find an exciting panorama of theories about the origin, nature, and meaning of evil. Those who study theodicy closely will discover recurring themes and arguments which form identifiable traditions within the general flow of Christian thought.[3] This chapter attempts to formulate a theodicy for our time, a response to the problem of gratuitous evil. Although some familiar theodicies are utilized, they are transformed by extending their implications to apply to the argument from gratuitous evil.

Free Will and Gratuitous Evil

An inveterate concept in Christian theodicy is that of free will. As long as God grants free will to mankind, there

2. L. Harold DeWolf, *A Theology of the Living Church*, rev. ed. (New York: Harper and Brothers, 1960), p. 130.

3. A number of authors have offered classificatory schemes for existing theodicies. See, e.g., John Hick, *Evil and the God of Love*, rev. ed. (New York: Harper and Row, 1975); and David Ray Griffin, *God, Power, and Evil: A Process Theodicy* (Philadelphia: Westminster, 1976). In terms of the kind of classification which emerges from the present book, most theodicies may be interpreted as attempts to reject either the theological premise or the factual premise.

is the unavoidable potential for moral evil. Furthermore, it can be argued that the concept of human free will includes not simply the possibility of bringing about evil, but the possibility of bringing about evil which is utterly gratuitous. If God is to bestow upon man a kind of freedom which is not just artificial but really significant, He must allow man a wide scope of choices and actions. Indeed, the kind of freedom which is basic to the accomplishment of great and noble actions is the kind of freedom which also allows the most atrocious deeds. In creating man and giving him free will, God thereby created an astonishing range of possibilities for both the creation and the destruction of value. Although some freely chosen evils sometimes have more disastrous consequences than intended, others seem to be motivated by the very desire to do irreparable damage. Perhaps this second kind of free choice is the true love of evil.

Among the possibilities open to man is that of freely choosing to bring about an utterly gratuitous evil. For God to prevent or eliminate all gratuitous evils in a meticulous way would be for Him to jeopardize the only kind of free will which can allow the human endeavor the highest significance. The very possibility of maximizing good is also the terrifying possibility of maximizing evil. Man possesses the awesome power either to create or to destroy things of value. This idea is not difficult to elucidate. God is the radical creator of a good world out of absolute nothing. He invested man with the responsibility of sharing in the enterprise of promoting positive value in the created order. Man can promote and enjoy positive values within this order only by living according to God's ordinances and by using divinely bestowed capacities. In a sense, then, the one thing which man can do which is most completely against God is to distort or eliminate positive values in God's economy—in effect, to become a radical destroyer.

The case that God allows gratuitous moral evil can perhaps be given strongest support by applying certain concepts from logical theory, much as Alvin Plantinga does in discussing free will.[4] Plantinga builds his argument upon the obvious principle that logically impossible states of affairs cannot be actual. From this he shows that it is not within God's power to *make* persons *freely* obey His will, for the very notion is self-contradictory. No doubt God can make people obey His will, but then they would not be doing so freely. Conversely, people can freely obey God's will, but then they are not being forced to do so by God. Thus, as long as God is to preserve the high value of free will, there are going to be some choices which are up to us, not God. There is no way, then, that God can insure that significantly free persons always choose and do what is right.

Plantinga's discussion of free will is sound as far as it goes. But it can be expanded further to cover the whole issue of whether God can allow *gratuitous* evil. Very simply, if the conception of human free will is taken to involve the possibility of bringing about really gratuitous evil (specifically, moral evil), then God cannot completely prevent or eliminate gratuitous evil without severely diminishing free will. That would be logically impossible. At stake here is not merely the ability of humans to choose among options, but the ability to choose among significant kinds of options: between goods and evils, even the highest goods and most terrible evils. Thus, free will is most significant—and most fitting for the special sort of creature man is—if it includes the potential for utterly damnable choices and actions. This is part of the inherent risk in God's program for man.

None of this is meant to imply that God always allows

4. Alvin Plantinga, *The Nature of Necessity* (New York: Oxford University, 1974), especially pp. 164–95.

men to carry out their most destructive intentions, since God overrides some human choices in order to accomplish His own general purposes. But God cannot always meticulously override human choices in order to prevent or eliminate their gratuitous effects and still protect a significant range of free will. The impact of all this for the problem of gratuitous evil can now be made explicit. Those authors who agree that God should allow man significant free will and who also insist that God must not allow any gratuitous evil (specifically, moral evil in this context) are unwittingly asking for the impossible.

One interesting benefit of this conception of gratuitous evil as a possibility which is *logically* linked to free will is that it does not necessitate limitation of any of the divine attributes, not even omnipotence. Philosophers widely agree that God's inability to bring about logically impossible states of affairs is no limitation on His power, since the logically impossible is really nothing at all. For example, Aquinas maintains that nothing which implies a contradiction falls under the scope of God's omnipotence.[5] And, as more recent philosophers (e.g., Plantinga) argue, the scope of omnipotence excludes not only those things which are logically impossible *in themselves* (e.g., married bachelors and square circles), but also those things which are logically possible in themselves but which are logically impossible *for God* to bring about (e.g., the free moral choices of finite agents).[6]

The present argument for the divine permission of gratuitous evil relies on this second type of logical consideration: it is logically impossible for God both to preclude the possibility of gratuitous moral evil and to preserve significant freedom. Absolutely speaking, of course, God

5. Thomas Aquinas, "How the Omnipotent God Is Said to Be Unable to Do Certain Things," in *The Power of God: Omnipotence and Evil*, ed. Linwood P. Urban and Douglas Walton (New York: Oxford University, 1978), pp. 54–58.

6. Plantinga makes this point in *Necessity*, p. 180.

does have the power to eliminate the possibility of gratuitous moral evil, but only if He withdraws significant freedom. This case for the possibility of gratuitous evil does not depend upon the imposition of metaphysical limitations (which are not logically necessitated) on God's power or any of His other attributes,[7] and hence is entirely compatible with traditional Christian theism.

Atheistic advocates of the principle of meticulous providence might well concede the seldom-noticed conceptual connection between free will and the possibility of gratuitous evil, but might modify the principle to raise a new objection. They might claim that, although God must allow some gratuitous evil in order to provide a significant domain of freedom, He should limit the degree of that freedom to avoid its particularly disastrous results. The charge against theism then becomes: God should not allow the great number and magnitude of gratuitous evils which exist or have existed, though admittedly He must allow some.[8]

The response to this objection is twofold. First, it is not clear that the objection takes into account the full meaning of the possibility of gratuitous evil. The whole idea that God created significant free will, and with it the possibility of gratuitous evil, seems to imply that there are no readily determined limits to that possibility. This point is not intended to suggest that God imposes no limits whatsoever on man and his affairs, since God obviously imposes various boundaries. However, it does stress the utter seriousness of what it is for mankind to possess significant freedom and with it the awesome possibility of

7. Authors who do argue for some nonlogical limits to God's power, goodness, or other attributes include Edgar Brightman and Alfred North Whitehead.

8. This kind of charge seems to be present in Edward Madden and Peter Hare, *Evil and the Concept of God* (Springfield, IL: Charles C. Thomas, 1968); e.g., on p. 3, where the phrase "so much *prima facie* gratuitous evil" is used.

creating gratuitous evil. Thus, things could get extremely bad as a result of the actualization of that possibility by free persons, and indeed they have. But this is commensurate with the possibility that important things might also be achieved by the actualization of the possibility for good. To remove or restrict the possibility of great evil is to remove or restrict proportionately the possibility of great good. This is the intolerable compliment which God has paid man by giving him significant free will.

Second, it appears that the issue regarding *how much* gratuitous evil God can allow depends upon personal judgment, not demonstration. This is a matter on which rational and moral persons may legitimately differ. A person whose value judgment is that God cannot allow *this much* evil to exist (i.e., the amount of evil the world actually contains) is going to have a problem embracing Christian theism. But the person whose value judgment differs may not have such a problem. It is crucial to recognize that the issue has proceeded beyond the point where theism itself is at stake. Instead the issue has become focused on the different standards which equally rational and moral persons may adopt. If this analysis is correct, then gratuitous evil in the world—not even in its most disturbing and prolific forms—does not necessarily pose an insurmountable theological or ethical problem for theism. Further objections regarding whether a world with this much gratuitous evil is worth it (i.e., worth God's creating at all) can be met with a similar reply.

The Relation Between the Moral and Natural Orders

Adaptation of free-will theodicy is not the only way to argue that God does not always demonstrate meticulous providence and hence that He can allow gratuitous evil. Natural-law theodicy can also be adapted to support the possibility of gratuitous evil. The argument may then focus either on the importance of a natural order to free will or on the character of a natural order itself. The first point generates further implications for gratuitous moral evil; the second has ramifications for gratuitous natural evil. This section examines the relation between the moral and natural orders, while the following section analyzes the concept of a natural system on its own terms.

Free will certainly seems to account for much gratuitous evil, specifically gratuitous moral evil. However, one condition for meaningful free will is seldom explored—that there must be some kind of natural order within which free creatures can operate. Free rational action requires a world of natural objects governed by natural laws. Such an order is essentially independent from the rational agent in that it consists of relatively enduring things behaving in regular ways. While talk of a natural order almost automatically suggests a physical realm, it also includes a psychological realm. What this independent order does is to provide a range of objects and actions as a field of deliberation and choice, a condition which is necessary to free will. Parts of this natural order can be manipulated to some extent by the free agent as a means of expressing his choice, another necessary condition of free will. If the objects in the world acted in sporadic and unpredictable ways, deliberation and action would be severely impaired if not eliminated. Furthermore, if the external objects in the world failed to respond, at least to some degree, to the internal commands of the will, meaningful choice and action would be precluded. Describing what a world would be without these conditions, Bruce Reichenbach writes: "There would be no regularity of sequence, no natural production of effects. But without the regularity which results from the governance of natural laws, rational action would be impossible."[9] It seems, then,

9. Bruce Reichenbach, "Natural Evils and Natural Laws: A Theodicy for Natural Evils," *International Philosophical Quarterly* 16 (1976): 187.

that the concept of free, rational activity is intimately linked to the concept of a natural system.

Of course, individual free will per se is not the only divine objective made possible by a natural system. God does not simply want an isolated individual interacting with a neutral environment, but also wants a society of free individuals interacting with each other in a variety of special ways. This kind of social structure once again demands a natural order as the context of common life. And since the natural order is to provide a neutral medium for interaction, it follows with even more force that it must have a fairly fixed and regular operation. C. S. Lewis makes this point in *The Problem of Pain:*

> As soon as we attempt to introduce the mutual knowledge of fellow-creatures we run up against the necessity of "Nature." People often talk as if nothing were easier than for two naked minds to "meet" or become aware of each other. But I see no possibility of their doing so except in a common medium which forms their "external world" or environment. . . . What we need for human society is exactly what we have—a neutral something, neither you nor I, which we can both manipulate so as to make signs to each other. . . . Society, then, implies a common field or "world" in which its members meet.[10]

We must now consider further implications of the concept of a natural world.

In providing the conditions for free action in general, a natural order, such as ours, thereby sets the stage for free moral action in particular. As F. R. Tennant poignantly states:

> It cannot be too strongly insisted that a world which is to be a moral order must be a physical order character-

10. C. S. Lewis, *The Problem of Pain* (New York: Macmillan, 1962), pp. 30–31.

ized by law or regularity. The theist is only concerned to invoke the fact that law-abidingness . . . is an essential condition of the world being a theatre of moral life. Without such regularity in physical phenomena there could be no probability to guide us: no prediction, no prudence, no accumulation of ordered experience, no pursuit of premeditated ends, no formation of habit, no possibility of character or of culture. Our intellectual faculties could not have developed. . . . And without rationality, morality is impossible.[11]

It is not difficult to argue that, in setting the stage for moral good, the natural order also sets the stage for moral evil. The very same framework which allows free will to be exercised in acts of respect, courtesy, modesty, charity, and love also allows free will to be expressed in acts of hostility, greed, cruelty, and hate. What must be added here is that significantly free will may express itself through the natural medium in evil actions which are utterly gratuitous. Hence, in providing an environment in which significant free will can operate, a natural order also provides the possibility of gratuitous moral evil.

Beyond this point, the exact borderline between moral and natural evils, or even gratuitous moral and natural evils, is hard to draw.[12] For example, an act of cruelty is a moral evil, but the physical pain it inflicts is a natural evil. Although there is no need to be extremely precise in drawing lines between moral and natural evils, we now have occasion to differentiate those natural evils which result from human causes and those which result from nonhuman causes. Whereas the above discussion emphasizes how a world order makes possible natural evil re-

11. F. R. Tennant, *Philosophical Theology*, 2 vols. (New York: Cambridge University, 1928), vol. 2, pp. 199–200.
12. See G. Wallace, "The Problems of Moral and Physical Evil," *Philosophy* 46 (1971): 349–51.

sulting from free human choice, we now turn our attention to how it makes possible natural evil produced by impersonal elements of the system itself. Examples of this are abundant: the same water which sustains and refreshes˙ can also drown; the same drug which relieves suffering can cause crippling psychological addiction; the same sun which gives light and life can parch fields and bring famine; the same neural arrangements which transmit intense pleasure and ecstasy can also bring extreme pain and agony.

As long as the objects in our world have relatively enduring natures operating according to relatively stable laws, which remain largely independent of our wills, the behavior of those objects cannot always be pleasing or good. So, not only does free will give rise to natural evils which are gratuitous (e.g., extreme, protracted physical suffering inflicted by an act of cruelty), but the natural system itself may do the same (e.g., extreme, protracted physical suffering caused by cancer). For God to eliminate the possibility of gratuitous natural evils arising from nonhuman causes is to eliminate a natural order altogether. But a natural order is required for the exercise of free will, as well as for a host of other things. The elimination of the possibility of gratuitous natural evils generated within the impersonal system may, therefore, be tantamount to the elimination of free will.

Natural Laws and Gratuitous Evil

Perhaps the claim that God cannot eliminate natural evils resulting from nonhuman causes does not seem as defensible as the earlier contention that He cannot eliminate natural evils resulting from free human choices. The critic might charge that God could change only those parts of the natural system which give rise to especially hideous or unjustified natural evils while leaving intact those other

parts which are necessary for free will and other worthwhile values. This charge may take either of two basic
forms, depending upon which method is recommended
for God's alteration of the natural order. Allegedly, God
could run the world either by miracle or by a different set
of laws, and thus avoid gratuitous evils which emerge
from the natural order itself. Under close scrutiny, however, it is not at all clear whether the critic can make
either form of the charge stick. Let us now examine the
charge that God could eliminate many, if not all, of the
gratuitous natural evils produced by nonhuman factors.
In the course of this examination, it will become obvious
that even these evils have close connections with important features of the world.

If the critic were to propose that it is possible for God
to intervene miraculously to prevent or eliminate pointless natural evils which arise within the world system,[13]
it would not be as difficult to answer him as some have
supposed. The first problem with the critic's suggestion
is that it appears to violate the concept of God's omniscience. Assuming for the moment that God is in the business of avoiding or removing pointless natural evils, His
omniscience would have foreseen them and arranged for
them to be avoided or removed from the beginning. There
would be no need for miraculous intervention to correct
or eliminate them.

A second problem with the critic's suggestion is that
even non–humanly-caused natural evils have an important bearing on the human drama. For instance, those
seemingly hopeless natural evils which call forth human
sympathy and moral effort, such as suffering and dis-
placement wrought by flood, hurricane, and fire, would
probably be absent in the critic's ideal world. The occa-

13. H. J. McCloskey makes this kind of proposal in "God and Evil," *The Philosophical Quarterly* 10 (1960): 97–114.

sions for a number of other virtues would probably be absent or greatly diminished as well. In short, the operation of the world would verge on becoming a sham, a trivialization of the environment in which outstanding achievement as well as real disaster can occur. So, just as God cannot eliminate gratuitous natural evils which are humanly caused without jeopardizing some very important features of human existence (e.g., free will), He cannot tamper with the gratuitous effects of the ongoing world order without also jeopardizing other high values.

Our response to the critic is not intended to preclude all possibility of miracle. Miracle, of course, has a place in the Christian religion, but not in the way the critic suggests. God's miraculous acts in history are not to eliminate meticulously every gratuitous evil, but to reveal something of utmost importance to His people or to act on their behalf. Such momentous miracles are often connected in various ways to the major doctrines of the faith. Then, too, there are the very rare times when God seems to work miracles in the private lives of believers. Unlike the systematic intervention proposed by the critic, both the historic and private miracles seem to be infrequent, and hence do not threaten the conditions of the natural order.

Pointing out the weaknesses of the critic's suggestion that God run the world by miraculous intervention does not totally dispel his attack. There is another way of formulating the charge that God could prevent non–humanly-caused gratuitous natural evils. The critic could say that, if God cannot reasonably remove gratuitous natural evils through miracle, He could instead have created a different natural system in which these evils would never have arisen in the first place.[14] Presumably, the critic is insisting

14. McCloskey, again, makes this kind of proposal in "The Problem of Evil," *Journal of Bible and Religion* 30 (1962), especially p. 191.

that God could have created an alternate natural world sufficiently like this one to contain all the good and beneficial things this one has (and possibly some of its more meaningful natural evils as well), but not contain any of the gratuitous natural evils this world does. Thus, it seems to the critic that God could at least have created a *better* natural world than this one. But again, the critic does not grasp the complex ramifications of what he is demanding. It is far from clear that a different set of natural laws could produce essentially the same good and approvable effects as the present ones do and yet not produce the ostensibly gratuitous evil consequences.

Let us now review this stronger way of formulating the critic's charge. Can God greatly reduce or eliminate pointless evils which result from the impersonal processes of the natural order simply by changing the laws by which it operates? First, it appears that the suggestion runs the risk of trivializing the context of free human action, and for many of the same reasons that the demand for miraculous intervention does. If natural laws operate in such a way as never to produce excessive evil, then the range of opportunities for certain virtues and vices would be greatly restricted. But opportunity for significant human action is not the only desirable feature in a natural world capable of producing gratuitous effects. Just to begin the list of other values, we might consider natural beauty. How well we know that many of the processes and objects of our world which sometimes display beauty are also the very ones which wreak havoc at other times.

There is a further problem with the critic's demand for a better natural system. Let us consider the notion that God can change natural laws which constitute the world order so as to eliminate their gratuitous effects and yet keep valuable objects and properties which exist in it. This assumption needs to be carefully analyzed. Natural laws are not abstract decrees which are forced upon the

objects of this world. Natural laws are descriptive statements about how the objects of this world act and react
under certain conditions. In short, it is the natural objects
of this world manifesting their own determinate natures
which form the basis of natural laws. Hence, there can be
no change in a system of natural laws without thereby
altering the natures of the objects within the system. But
if alteration of the prevailing natural laws entails alteration of the relevant natural objects, we cannot be sure
what kind of world we would have or how its value would
compare to that of the present world. Something called
fire whose nature was no longer to burn when put in con-
tact with skin would not be like any fire we know. Sentient creatures who cannot feel pain would not partake of
the sentient existence we share with other animals. The
point might be pressed even further to show that nothing
which we now call "human" could exist in such a world.

At this point, the critic may protest that his initial suggestion regarding a better natural system has been grossly
exaggerated and then conveniently dismissed. But this is
not the case. We have simply tried to take the proposed
change in the natural system seriously, and have drawn
out implications which the critic might not have foreseen.
When the critic requires "only a small change" in the
present set of natural laws in order to avoid their gratuitous evil consequences, he might not realize how great a
change is involved. Since almost all natural objects are
capable of producing harmful as well as beneficial results,
virtually all natural laws would have to be modified, with
the correlative modification of virtually all natural objects. Even the slightest modification may produce manifold and intricate differences between this present natural
order and the envisioned one. The whole matter becomes
so complex that no finite mind can conceive of precisely
what modifications the envisioned natural world would
have to incorporate in order both to preserve the good

natural effects and to avoid the fortuitous evil ones. And if the desired modifications cannot be detailed, then the further task of conceiving how the proposed natural world is better than this present one seems patently impossible. However, it is not just our human finitude which seems to undercut the critic's case, since the critic might always presume that an omniscient deity could conceive of such changes. It is simply the character of any set of natural laws to occasion both good and evil. Therefore, it is not clear that even God can modify the natural system we have in order to remove its evil and destructive effects but retain its good and desirable effects.

None of what has been said in defense of the natural order[15] in which so much gratuitous evil is produced implies that this is the best of all possible worlds or that it is the only world God could have created. Rather, what has been said is an attempt to show that the existence of a natural order in general is a necessary condition for free will and a host of other goods. Furthermore, it ventures the thesis that something very much like *this* natural order is a necessary condition of having the exact goods we have. So, contrary to the critic's rejoinders, it may well be that God cannot remove the gratuitous evils of this world and still preserve its goods or the opportunities for those goods.

The conclusion, then, is that God cannot eliminate the frightening possibility of gratuitous natural evil as long as He chooses to sustain natural order which, in turn, sustains a great many natural and moral goods. C. S. Lewis has words exactly to the point:

The inexorable "laws of Nature" which operate in defiance of human suffering or desert, which are not turned

15. Reichenbach, "Natural Evils," and Lewis, *Pain*, are extremely helpful on the concept of the natural system and deserve careful study.

aside by prayer, seem at first sight to furnish a strong argument against the goodness and power of God. I am going to submit that not even Omnipotence could create a society of free souls without at the same time creating a relatively independent and "inexorable" Nature.[16]

If the above considerations regarding a natural world order are correct, then gratuitous natural evils do not pose an insurmountable problem for Christian theism. Not only are real and potential gratuitous natural evils not a devastating problem for a theistic perspective, but, properly understood, they are a part of a world order which seems to be precisely the kind God *would* create to provide for certain goods. We must now investigate more fully the claim that *this* is the kind of world which an omniscient, omnipotent, wholly good God would create.

Gratuitous Evil and Soul-Making

In the preceding sections, it has been argued that the existence of utterly destructive, pointless evils does not constitute an unanswerable question for Christian theism. Such evils, whether moral or natural, raise a problem only when it is assumed that God exhibits meticulous providence, that He assiduously prevents or eliminates all gratuitous evil within His creation. However, this assumption can be seen to be untenable when the full meanings of free moral order and natural order are taken seriously. Whereas the assumption of (MP) initially seemed to be implied by some basic ethical and theological principles, it has now been shown that (MP) is not a necessary conclusion from these principles at all. In fact, at least the possibility of gratuitous evil seems implied by some of our deepest commitments about what the moral and nat-

16. Lewis, *Pain*, p. 29; see also Peter T. Geach, *Providence and Evil* (New York: Cambridge University, 1977), chapter 6.

ural orders must be. If this is so, the argument that gratuitous evil supplies telling evidence against Christian theism is severely weakened.

However, in addition to the inherently negative task of defense, an adequate response to the argument from gratuitous evil should attempt the positive task of giving reasons why Christian theism is credible even in light of gratuitous evil. Ironically, central concepts in the rebuttal of the atheistic argument suggest that gratuitous evil may be fashioned into a case for the truth of Christian theism. In the remaining pages of this chapter, these concepts are developed to show that gratuitous evil (both potential and actual) supports the truth of a theistic world-view. First, in this section, we will consider how gratuitous evil figures into the process of soul-making. Second, we will see how gratuitous evil illumines certain Christian doctrines. Third, we will develop an apologetic of creation vis-à-vis gratuitous evil.

There is little debate over the claim that God's primary purpose in creation is to bring forth mature moral and rational creatures. Briefly, then, God is interested in soul-making. There are some highly valuable traits which God wants each soul to possess. For example, each human being should be capable of acting virtuously toward others and of exercising faith and love toward God. Now it is plausible that only certain kinds of environments (and not others) are conducive to producing such beings. Theorizing about what kind of environment would be most conducive, John Hick argues that it must include real challenges and risks in order to evoke creativity and achievement, present significant opportunities for the development of virtue and character, and be located at a sufficient distance from God to allow man autonomy.[17] Hick seems correct in saying that these conditions are

17. Hick, *Evil*, pp. 243–91.

found only in a world in which there is genuinely gratuitous evil and the haunting possibility of further gratuitous evil. A world in which total failure and ruin are ruled out is sterilized of all meaningful challenges. A world in which there is no extreme hardship, innocent suffering, or unjust treatment calls forth little moral effort, sympathy, and other valuable human traits. Moreover, a world which is obviously filled with the presence of God would very probably overwhelm man's intellect and will in such a way as to coerce him into religious belief.

While Hick's line of reasoning is generally correct, the notion of the necessity of man's distance from God deserves special comment. For Hick, human freedom with respect to God presupposes a degree of separateness or independence from God. This is the concept of *epistemic distance*, by which Hick means that "the reality and presence of God must not be borne in upon men in the coercive way in which their natural environment forces itself upon their attention. The world must be to man, to some extent at least, . . . as if there were no God."[18] So the world must initially conceal God and reveal Him only to those who seek Him in faith and love. At one point Hick quotes Ralph Cudworth for support: "It is in itself fit, that there should be somewhere a doubtful and cloudy state of things, for the better exercise of virtue and faith."[19]

Particularly relevant for present purposes is the fact that, whatever else might contribute to the ambiguous or even nontheistic appearance of the world, both the actuality and possibility of gratuitous evil play an important role. Such evils form a part of the total context in which man is embedded and in which the desired epistemic distance from the Creator is provided. Hence, to the extent that epistemic distance is a condition of free religious de-

18. Ibid., p. 281.
19. Ibid., p. 334.

votion, the horrible and devastating evils which help create that context cannot be ruled out.

Hick associates a number of additional claims with the one regarding epistemic distance. For instance, from the concept of epistemic distance he concludes that the fall of man was "virtually inevitable": "man's spiritual location at an epistemic distance from God makes it virtually inevitable that man will organize his life apart from God and in self-centered competitiveness with his fellows. How can he be expected to center his life upon a Creator who is as yet unknown to him?"[20] Extending this idea, Hick claims that the fall is prerequisite to coming to God in free and loving obedience: "God is so overwhelmingly great that the children in His heavenly family must be prodigal children who have voluntarily come to their Father from a far country."[21] Of course, the concept of epistemic distance can be analyzed in different ways. Contrary to Hick's line of thinking, one need not take the concept of epistemic distance to entail that the fall is practically inevitable or logically necessary. The basic concept of epistemic distance can be used simply to accent important characteristics of our creaturely existence without adopting Hick's additional claims.

An intriguing contrast to—and perhaps ultimately a complement to—Hick's idea that gratuitous evil contributes to man's epistemic distance from God is the idea that even the most negative and destructive elements of our world can also be construed as an epistemic avenue to God. Romans 1:20 declares that the invisible nature of God is clearly seen in the created world. The prospect is tantalizing that perhaps this vision of God is available in and through the worst evils of our world as well as in the manifold goods. In other words, if the theistic world-view

20. Ibid., p. 286.
21. Ibid., p. 323.

includes both possible and actual gratuitous evils, then these evils tend to count as evidence for, rather than against, its truth.

If we conceive God as a fastidious cosmic potentate who arranges the goods and evils of this world into neat and simple patterns, certainly this God will seem hidden from us and any brand of theism built on this conception will be falsified. Such a concept of deity can hardly account for the complex and frustrating admixture of good and evil in the world, and the times when evil emerges as the dominant force. It is not surprising that the modern age, preoccupied with the meaningless and absurd features of our world, is quick to pronounce this simplistic God "silent," "absent," and even "dead." One natural defense against this pronouncement has been to reinterpret or deny our ordinary experience of evil. This seems to be a rather high price to pay in order to salvage an oversimplified conception of deity.

Some contemporary theologians have sought to preserve the integrity of experience by modifying the traditional Christian concept of God. But this tack typically impoverishes the idea of God to the extent that it ceases to be conceptually adequate or theologically acceptable. What we need, therefore, is a concept of the Christian God which is capable of covering not just the manageable evils of life but the severe and hopeless evils as well.

Frederick Sontag undertakes to develop such a concept in *The God of Evil: An Argument from the Existence of the Devil*. Sontag proposes that "we start . . . from the accumulated negative elements [of the world] and build from them an account of a God who can exist in spite of such destructive forces—one whose existence is commensurate with the presence of strong negativity."[22] Sontag's pro-

22. Frederick Sontag, *The God of Evil: An Argument from the Existence of the Devil* (New York: Harper and Row, 1970), p. 4.

posal need not be taken as a plea for weakening the orthodox conception of deity, say, to the point of making
God so benign as never to combat evil. Neither does his
proposal have to be taken as bidding us to draw up an
eclectic picture of God from all sorts of disparate experiences so that it cannot be falsified by any of them. For
present purposes, Sontag's point (or something similar)
can function as a fruitful suggestion for fashioning gratuitous evil into a positive case for theism. Rather than
being an epistemic obstacle to God, gratuitous evil might
provide a sort of epistemic access to Him.

Some of the relevant components of an adequate picture of God have been advanced in the prior discussions
of free will and natural law. When we consider that God
chose to create free rational and moral agents who would
exist in an independent, stable order—even though this
creation entails the possibility of gratuitous evil—we see
a God who places a high premium on creativity, moral
effort, and related goods. We see a God who does not hes-
itate to permit conditions (e.g., a natural order within
which free creatures can significantly operate) under which
such goods can be achieved, even though these same conditions may give some men grounds for atheism. We find
a God who seeks to transform creatures progressively into
His likeness, even if this process can occur only in a radically contingent world which may incline men to reject
Him. Of course, these observations form only the beginning of a concept of God which can account for gratuitous
evil.

Gratuitous Evil and Doctrinal Considerations

Up to this point, the overall argument has been that
the principle of meticulous providence is not tenable, and
hence that it cannot be employed in the evidential argument from gratuitous evil. For far too long this dubious

principle has simply been assumed to be a corollary of fundamental theological and moral beliefs. But it has now been shown that theology and morality do not necessitate this principle; it has been argued that God's relation to evil is quite different from what the principle of meticulous providence requires. The points elaborated above—which revolve around the risk of free will, the maintenance of a natural order, and the program of soul-making—show that God's permission of gratuitous evil is entirely faithful to a theistic understanding of the world. To approach this thesis from a slightly different angle, consider what the divine permission of gratuitous evil implies for certain theological and moral concepts. The present section shows how several Christian doctrines are enhanced by the denial that God is a meticulous providence. The next section shows that our understanding of the whole moral enterprise is enriched by recognizing that God can allow gratuitous evil.

The recognition that (MP) is unacceptable and thus that God allows gratuitous evil opens up new vistas of understanding God's way with the world. The doctrine of the fall and the doctrine of redemption are, for example, augmented by the recognition of gratuitous evil. The concept of the fall is enhanced by including the notion that man exercised not merely a capability for evil, but a radical capability for gratuitous evil. God cannot remove all of the gratuitous evil which man creates and still maintain the significance of the human venture. The resultant lostness of the world, then, is not a condition which can be completely annihilated or compensated by temporal goods or the goods of the coming kingdom. Hence, a complete conception of what it is to have a lost world includes the utter pointlessness of some evil.

Following the logic of what it is for the world to be lost leads eventually to the concept of what it is for the world to be redeemed. In light of the foregoing argument against

(MP), God's plan of redemption need not be conceived as primarily a program for meticulously compensating for every evil *event* or *situation* which has ever occurred, though redemption will undoubtedly include goods which far outweigh many past evils. We must realize that God's main objective is to redeem *persons*, rational and moral souls, whose lives have been affected by those evils. And the nature of that redemption, whether in its current progress or future culmination, is more profound and splendid than the principle of meticulous providence captures. It involves a fulfilment of personhood in the presence of God which does not depend upon whether every temporal evil is requited. In this sense Romans 8:28 can affirm that "in everything God works for good with those who love Him."

Adoption of the principle of meticulous providence frequently creates a compulsion to rid theology of the doctrine of hell. Remember that (MP) is generally taken to specify how an omnipotent, omniscient, wholly good deity deals with evil. And, by extrapolation, the utter lostness of hell is often conceived—though not always in just these terms—to be a gratuitous evil which God must ultimately eliminate.[23] But the more clearly it is seen that Christian theism does not imply (MP), the easier it becomes to accept the doctrine of hell.

It cannot be demonstrated that God is obliged to eliminate the gratuitous evils which man has an awesome power to create. Furthermore, it is reasonable to believe that the terrifying human potential for evil includes the possibility of some person's willing and loving evil to the extent that hell becomes the emergent, dominant choice of his whole life. Hell is simply the natural culmination of things which he has voluntarily set in motion. Just as

23. John Hick, e.g., states that God will empty hell by His infinite seeking love *(Evil,* p. 242).

God cannot override a person's every evil choice, He cannot contravene the larger, cumulative evil orientation of one's life. If God is going to allow us to exist as significantly free beings, capable of the highest achievements, then He must allow us also the most depraved and senseless errors—even if they lead to hell. Hell is the logical extension of the idea that man has the radical power to create gratuitous evil.

There is no need here to give a complete analysis of the nature of hell. Of course, the concept of hell is troublesome, and previous arguments do not hang on the present reference to it, which is simply to point out that the divine permission of gratuitous evil helps remove certain apparent inconsistencies between the doctrine of hell and other standard theological and moral beliefs. Beyond the initial connection between gratuitous evil and hell, much more remains to be discussed to bring the doctrine of hell into proper focus.

Gratuitous Evil and the Creation of the Moral Context

The preceding analysis traces the theological implications of the concept that God allows gratuitous evil, but has not emphasized the moral implications of the concept. To acknowledge the divine permission of pointless evil is to imply that (MP) is not a necessary truth of ethics. The central question, then, can be posed as follows: "Granted that a world in which gratuitous evil can occur is God's plan, is it really worth it?" This issue concerns whether the possible and actual goods which exist in this world are worth the horrendous evils which exist. And if the whole enterprise is not somehow worth it, then God seems to be, in a real sense, immoral.

How can God's creation of the world be squared with refined moral insight? Perhaps the issue here, as some extreme critics have seen, can be pressed to the limit: "Should God have created at all?" It has already been shown that it is outside of God's power to eliminate gratuitous evil as long as He protects free will, a natural order, and a soul-making environment. But the clear insinuation in the critics' question is that it would have been morally preferable to forego the goods of this world and thereby avoid the evils.[24]

An argument constructed out of these concerns might run as follows. God's morality must be somehow continuous with ours. If God violates our highest and best moral values, then surely He is no better than an omnipotent fiend. In creating this world with all its terrible evil, it appears that God proves Himself to be a fiend, causing or permitting evils on a scale which no human villain could match. This condemnation of God's choice to create the present world can be motivated from either a teleological or a deontological position, but it shall be discussed here without making that distinction. We will see that, contrary to what the critics' rhetoric might suggest, God cannot be accused of violating our moral convictions in creating and sustaining the world. In fact, God's relation to the world is in full accord with our most cherished values.

The attempt to accuse God of violating our moral principles suffers, it seems, from a peculiar form of anthropomorphism. While it is quite right to say that God's morality must be broadly consistent with ours,[25] it is misleading to say that He is just one moral agent among other moral agents, and therefore that He must be judged on exactly the same terms. Naturally, God's morality cannot be sheerly different from ours, say, as black from white, without eliciting our moral repugnance. But there are some very special considerations which apply to God as

24. This claim is not merely insinuated but defended in Richard LaCroix, "Unjustified Evil and God's Choice," *Sophia* 13 (1974): 20–28.
25. See Lewis, *Pain*, pp. 37–39.

the creator of a moral context, and these considerations prevent Him from acting as just any other agent within that context.

God is not content merely to contemplate and approve the realm of moral absolutes; He desires to maintain a whole society of moral agents who can do so as well, a society of free souls who can cultivate vital moral life. As we have seen, this means that God cannot guarantee that the moral thing is always done. The real question becomes whether God's failing to provide a guarantee that the good will be done makes Him morally blameworthy. Let us ponder for a moment whether our moral structures can condemn the very being who makes it possible for us even to exist, to be able to apprehend moral values in the first place, and to have the significance of life which is lived within their ambit. Of course, we morally condemn those who lie, steal, and murder, but it is not at all clear that we must likewise condemn God for creating the context in which such evils can happen. Surely it accords with the very spirit of morality for God to create a moral context and a plurality of finite beings living within it. At the heart of morality is the principle that we should not merely avoid evil but should also seek good. We must see creation itself, then, as the supreme expression of the moral impulse to create something good, indeed to create a whole context within which finite agents are capable of achieving various goods. Is this creation not, as the Book of Genesis records, "very good"?

Technically, the creation of a moral context might be called a second-order good, since it is a necessary condition for positive first-order goods.[26] The Christian tradi-

---

26. It should not be mistakenly assumed that justification of the creation of a moral context is thereby justification of all evils which arise within it. A moral context requires only the possibility of moral evil, not the actuality. Hence, the reality of genuinely gratuitous evil is preserved: some actual evils are simply not *necessary*.

tion teaches that only God can produce this great and marvelous panorama of opportunities for the human attainment of good. Hence, contrary to the opinion of many critics, God's morality is not less, but is more, than our own. God's morality is greater than ours in that it makes possible our highest moral aspirations and gives us the privilege of either succeeding or failing in their pursuit. God's bestowal of moral life on finite creatures, therefore, is indeed moral. It is moral at the most profound level. This is why there is not much force in the objection that it would have been better if God had not created. Better for whom? Surely not for us, since we would not exist and the whole moral enterprise would not be under way.

Following this line of thought from morality back to theology helps us understand that God's creation of the world is a manifestation of grace and His continued maintenance of the world an act of mercy. The orthodox Christian tradition affirms that God did not create out of metaphysical necessity, as some philosophical systems hold (e.g., Neo-Platonism). And Christian theology holds that God did not create in order to gain something for Himself, such as worship or fellowship, as some misinterpretations of the tradition suggest. The resounding declaration throughout centuries of Christian thought is that God created in order to give, not to get. The gift He has given, however, is a perilous one, making possible both man's grandeur and his shame. Now, the persistent critic may not like it that God created such a world as this, but he can express this thought only as a personal preference and not as an indictment emerging from the very heart of morality, for we have already seen otherwise.

If this brief scenario of creation is correct, then God's perfect goodness is not impugned by the existence of gratuitous evil in the world. The scenario denies that either theology or morality requires a meticulous providence which busily prevents or eliminates all gratuitous evils, or refrains from creating in order to avoid their possibility.

So far, it has been argued that the divine permission of gratuitous evil is both theologically and morally acceptable. But it can be further argued that the permission of gratuitous evil by the God of Christian theism is the best explanation of the perplexing world we face. This is a much stronger claim. It means that an interpretation of Christian theism which includes gratuitous evil not only is consistent with our best theological and moral insights, but is the most appropriate and compelling exemplification of these insights. Christian theism is the best account of the facts of our religious and ethical experience. Only a world with the theistic origin and structure described in this chapter is capable of containing the kind of gratuitous evils we observe.

Only in a game in which the stakes are incredibly high and the conditions for winning so precarious is it possible to lose in the tragic and inexplicable ways we do. The theistic character of the world provides our highest opportunities and yet makes possible our worst defeats. Alluding to William Makepeace Thackeray's phrase, Peter Geach calls God "the Ordainer of the lottery" and explains the great risk of the human adventure:

> Our freedom is our supreme dignity; that makes us children of the Most High; we can enjoy it only by living in a partly chancy world—and that means a world in which there will be goods and evils of fortune distributed according to the laws of chance. We have no choice but to enter for the lottery; and we are able by taking thought to learn its terms. . . . We cannot opt out of the lottery nor alter its terms; and it is vain to look *here* for distributive or retributive justice; it is only that the Ordainer of the lottery plays fair.[27]

27. Geach, *Providence*, p. 120.

We could add an array of concepts to the concept of free will employed in Geach's statement. These additional concepts shed further light on the awesome possibility of gratuitous evil in this radically contingent world: conceptions of natural law and soul-making just begin the list. All of these factors together constitute a kind of profound justice in the unalterable conditions of human existence, a justice which, properly understood, is not easily faulted.

This chapter explores the concepts of free will, natural law, and soul-making, and shows how they exclude a strict principle of meticulous providence. In fact, when we draw the implications of these concepts for a plausible theodicy and theory of creation, an unexpected irony surfaces in the rebuttal of the argument from gratuitous evil. The atheistic argument under consideration turns on the notion that theism implies an altogether different reality from the one we experience. However, in the course of the rebuttal, Christian theism is shown to include, not exclude, gratuitous evil.[28] It appears, therefore, that *this* is exactly the kind of world one would expect to find if theism is true. Alternative conceptual systems, such as naturalism or pantheism, can explain neither our peculiar consciousness of value nor its senseless destruction.[29] The character of the goods and evils of this world, then, actually tends to confirm theism, not disconfirm it, as the

28. Christian theism is a complex unity of doctrine which must be viewed in its entirety. Some critics have treated certain aspects of the doctrine in isolation from others and have generated spurious conclusions. The principle of meticulous providence is one of these.

29. Of course, naturalism and pantheism do provide explanations of good and evil in the world. However, these explanations do not seem to capture the precise nature of good and evil in human experience. Naturalism typically cannot account for the ultimate and absolute character which we ascribe to values. Pantheism cannot explain why good and evil should be in conflict within the very life of God. Further pursuit of these and other criticisms proves to be a fascinating study.

atheistic critic supposes. Thus, the present response to the
problem of gratuitous evil has two aspects. The first aspect is the refutation of the initial atheistic argument. The
second aspect is the development of an argument for
theism based on gratuitous evil.

To summarize, our refutation of the evidential argument from gratuitous evil can be depicted by referring to
the inductive model of disconfirmation developed earlier:

1. If (G) is true, then, assuming that (MP) is true,
   ($\sim$E$_3$) should be true.   (theological premise)
2. It is probable that (E$_3$) is true.   (factual premise)
3. Therefore, it is probable that (G) is false.   (logical conclusion)

Since we have now rejected (MP), the first premise does
not hold and the argument cannot go through. Hence, the
atheistic conclusion simply cannot be drawn. Thus, the
principal burden of this chapter—to offer an effective rebuttal of the evidential argument from gratuitous evil—
is accomplished.

But the process of rebuttal itself suggests a new argument for theism based on the evidence of gratuitous evil.
Contrary to the atheistic idea that gratuitous evil provides
evidence which disconfirms theism, we now see that such
evil supplies evidence which tends to confirm theism. The
key to this turnabout lies in the rejection of the principle
of meticulous providence. It was this principle which made
gratuitous evil seem to constitute negative evidence in the
first place (by stipulating that gratuitous evil cannot occur
in a theistic universe). However, in examining the reasons
why the principle must be denied, and thus how it is that
God can legitimately allow some gratuitous evils, the way
was opened for a better understanding of God's relation
to the world. Perhaps this more plausible understanding

could be distilled into what we might call the principle of gratuitous evil:

> (PG) An omnipotent, omniscient, wholly good God could allow gratuitous or pointless evil.

With this new principle, the original theological premise in the evidential argument from gratuitous evil can be totally revised. And with the revised theological premise, which incorporates (PG), the evidential argument can be transformed in favor of theism. Instead of the atheistic argument with which we started, we get the beginnings of a theistic argument from gratuitous evil:

1. If (G) is true, then, assuming that (PG) is true, (E_3) could be true.   (revised theological premise)
2. It is probable that (E_3) is true.   (factual premise)
3. Therefore, it is probable that (G) is true.   (logical conclusion)

This argument turns on the belief that theism implies that gratuitous evil is at least possible in a theistic world. Since there are good reasons to think that gratuitous evil is actual, then it is obviously possible. Hence, the existence of gratuitous evil tends to confirm the brand of Christian theism which countenances it. Remarkably, given the interpretation of theism offered in this chapter, (E_3) supplies some degree of supporting evidence for (G)—exactly the opposite of what the atheistic challenger intends. This new theistic argument conforms to the inductive model of confirmation explained in chapter 3, and thus provides reasonable grounds for belief in theism.

Of course, further analysis is needed to determine the exact weight of the suggested theistic argument from gratuitous evil and its relation to other arguments in the overall debate on theism. For example, the theist who wants to argue this line will eventually have to show that the existence and insidious character of the gratuitous evils of this world do not confirm important nontheistic options (e.g., naturalism). However, the present sketch of the theistic argument from gratuitous evil suffices to show that, even in the face of the most horrible evils, Christian theism has the ring of truth.

6

The Existential Problem of Evil

The Neglected Dimension of the Problem of Evil

The experience of evil is a fundamental and pervasive feature of human existence. However, contemporary thinkers often seem unable to articulate the exact nature of the problem as it occurs in ordinary life. Professional philosophers typically discuss the problem of evil as a technical and logical dilemma, and thereby remove it from the grasp of many laymen.[1] Theologians, on the other hand, currently tend to treat the problem as an emotional dilemma and thereby neglect its rational impact.[2] Writers on both sides have been polarized, each side insisting that the other is insensitive to important aspects of the problem. While there is no question that abstract reflection is crucial to solving the problem of evil, and that emotional responses to evil cannot be ignored, the problem as a whole is not exclusively cognitive or exclusively emotive.

There is a dimension of the problem of evil in which thought, feeling, and volition coalesce, a response which reflects a total sense of life. This might appropriately be

1. This abstract dilemma is essentially the logical version of the problem of evil (see chapter 2).
2. The emotional response to the problem of evil is discussed on pp. 40–43.

called the existential dimension of the problem of evil. Yet this problem cannot be described as a simple juxtaposition of the logical and emotional responses to evil. Now that the evidential argument from gratuitous evil has been identified as an important theoretical expression of the problem, we have a fresh clue as to the real existential impact of the problem. Furthermore, the solutions previously offered for the theoretical argument from gratuitous evil suggest ways of handling the existential question of gratuitous evil.

Our analysis is divided into three phases. First, we will determine precisely what the experience of evil is, particularly the experience of gratuitous evil. Second, we will explore fitting ways to cope with or respond to the sense of evil in human existence. Third, we will study how the experience of evil—even gratuitous evil—functions within the total context of commitment to a Christian worldview and way of life.

Religious Commitment and the Meaning of Evil

The setting of Albert Camus's novel *The Plague* is the Algerian town of Oran, which is stricken by a deadly epidemic. As the townspeople begin to realize the seriousness of the disaster which has befallen them, they raise the timeless question of why God allows such evil to exist. Father Paneloux, a Jesuit priest, is asked to deal with this question in a sermon to the people. In his opening words, Father Paneloux issues a harsh accusation: "Calamity has come to you, my brethren, and, my brethren, you deserved it."[3] He charges that the people have been lax in their obedience to God and have brought the plague upon themselves as punishment. The priest goes on to explain

3. Albert Camus, *The Plague*, trans. Stuart Gilbert (New York: Random House, 1948), pp. 86–87.

that God has ordained the entire scheme of things, the evil as well as the good, "wrath and pity; the plague and your salvation."[4] And he maintains that God's purposes are hidden in His supreme reason, which cannot be questioned by puny human minds.

After preaching this sermon, Paneloux joins a team whose job is to care for those who are suffering and dying. But while serving on the team, Paneloux witnesses the agonizing death of an innocent child. Paneloux and Doctor Rieux, who is very likely Camus's protagonist, attend the child throughout the night. Upon the child's death, Rieux turns to Paneloux and exclaims fiercely, "Ah! That child, anyhow, was innocent, and you know it as well as I do!"[5] Paneloux's reply to Rieux reiterates the appeal to God's transcendent reason which humanity cannot fathom: "That sort of thing is revolting because it passes our human understanding. But perhaps we should love what we cannot understand."[6]

Obviously there is much to discuss in Camus's disturbing tale.[7] The dogmatic defense of evil—by citing the retributive theory, appealing to a greater future harmony, and ultimately resorting to the inscrutable divine wisdom—merits careful and sustained discussion. However, all of these maneuvers simply reflect the underlying conviction that all evils are somehow meaningful and justified. In other words, they are simply concrete applications of the principle of meticulous providence. The implication of such thinking, as we have seen, is that there is really no gratuitous evil in the world. In the case of Father Paneloux, the suffering of the innocent child had to have some justification, even though he is driven to confess that

4. Ibid., p. 90.
5. Ibid., p. 196.
6. Ibid.
7. See Ben Mijuskovic, "Camus and the Problem of Evil," *Sophia* 15 (1976): 11–19.

perhaps only God knows what it is. The powerful lesson which emerges here can be generalized to cover many other cases in which the principle of meticulous providence is dogmatically accepted. What Camus seems to suggest, using the figure of Paneloux, is that as long as one believes that there is no genuinely gratuitous evil, he will tend to deny or distort the import of his actual experience of the world. After his earlier claims about the punitive nature of the plague, Paneloux could not squarely face the clear innocence of the child. Likewise, many religious believers who adopt (consciously or unconsciously) some version of the principle of meticulous providence on the conceptual level have great difficulty accepting the experience of gratuitous evil as veridical.

When one recognizes the tension between the theoretical commitment to meticulous providence, on the one hand, and the existential perception of gratuitous evil, on the other hand, he has only a few basic options for removing that dissonance. If he takes the principle of meticulous providence to be absolutely essential to Christian theism, then he may either revise other parts of theism in light of the experience of gratuitous evil, or reinterpret his experience in light of the categories he attributes to theism. Many contemporary theodicists tend to take the former route, promising a new account of theism which is faithful to human experience. Traditional theodicists tend to go the latter route and thus construe every evil as necessarily having some meaning or justification. And those thinkers who do not think it possible to revise theism adequately or to reinterpret experience sufficiently tend to reject theism altogether.

Perhaps Sidney Hook explains the tension best by saying that "no religion which conceives of God as both omnipotent and benevolent, no metaphysics which asserts that the world is rational, necessary and good has any

room for genuine tragedy."[8] Tragedy, for Hook, is roughly
equivalent to what we are calling gratuitous evil. And
Hook is right insofar as he is referring to any religion
which assumes that God is a fastidious deity who always
makes things turn out for the best. One who adheres to
such a religious orientation is usually unable to accept
genuine tragedy. This rejection of genuine tragedy takes
place not only on the conceptual level, but, consequently,
on the experiential level as well. Erazim Kohák notes:
"Christians, specifically, have regularly been accused of
a constitutional inability to grasp the reality of tragedy
because of their confidence in the ultimate victory of good
over evil."[9] Kohák proceeds to explain how theological
affirmations may be used as emotional opiates to assuage
the experience of tragedy.

Conceptual Structure and the Experience of Gratuitous Evil

What we have come to is the realization that one's conceptual commitments condition the range and quality of
his experience. As we have already seen, one's adherence
to certain theological perspectives reduces the likelihood
that he will perceive the full impact of tragedy in the
world. Based on such perspectives, which characteristically involve the principle of meticulous providence, the
tendency is to reinterpret the data of experience in such
a way as to deny that there are gratuitous evils. Chapter
4 cautioned against undue reconstruction of experience
and thus advised acceptance of the factual premise in the
theoretical arguments from gratuitous evil. This paved

8. Sidney Hook, *Pragmatism and the Tragic Sense of Life* (New York: Basic
Books, 1974), p. 18.
9. Erazim Kohák, "The Person in a Personal World: An Inquiry into the
Metaphysical Significance of the Tragic Sense of Life," *Independent Journal
of Philosophy* 1 (1977): 60.

the road for a different answer to the argument. In the current discussion, it is likewise recommended that the facts of gratuitous evil be accepted, but for reasons which now pertain to the experiential domain of the problem of evil. The motivation here is that the experience of tragedy and gratuitous evil is an important aspect of the human condition. Hence, any set of conceptual categories which tends to exclude gratuitous evil diminishes the sense of evil and thereby a crucial aspect of the human venture. When the experience of gratuitous evil is accepted as generally valid, and the principle of meticulous providence is relinquished, one may reap both conceptual and experiential benefits. In the previous chapters, we discovered conceptual benefits for theology when pointless and tragic evils are admitted. Let us now investigate the experiential advantages for theism.

The experience of the tragic undoubtedly has a complex and intricate phenomenological structure which cannot be fully described in a few pages. Nevertheless, there are several aspects of this experience which have implications for the overall problem of gratuitous evil, and thus merit attention here. Before proceeding, it must be emphasized that the whole notion of experience is problematic in many respects. For example, the concept of experience is ambiguous with respect to its temporal characteristics. It is equally legitimate to speak of "the experience of pain upon stubbing one's toe" and to speak of "the experience of living in a foreign country," expressions which do not denote comparable temporal boundaries. Other ambiguous features of the concept of experience could be readily enumerated. However, the present focus on the experience of the tragic will not be its problematic aspects, but those aspects of it which seem clear and essential.

A central point here is that there is an intimate interplay between reason and emotion in human experience in general and in the experience of tragedy in particular.

Any experience, even that of the tragic, is largely a product of these two factors. There is a prevailing opinion that reason and emotion are alien to one another. But the best of philosophical anthropology suggests that there is a close relation between the two. An emotion has no meaning without some conceptual interpretation being placed upon it. One's conceptual commitments antecedently condition the quality of one's emotions, and determine one's consequent reflection upon them.

It is important, then, that we recognize the almost organic unity between thought and feeling as we examine the experience of tragedy. To speak of this experience is not only to express an emotion about the terrible pangs of life felt in the presence of evil, but also to communicate something of the meaning of those feelings—a meaning which derives from more general and abstract conceptual commitments. Two persons who possess very different conceptual schemes frequently assign quite different significance to what might otherwise seem to be similar experiences. This is why theists who accept the principle of meticulous providence cannot fully experience the horrendous evils of our world. But if one admits the real possibility of gratuitous evil into his conceptual interpretation of the world, his experience of much evil is radically altered. In the following paragraphs, a proposal is made regarding what appear to be the prominent characteristics of the experience of gratuitous evil, taking into account the fact that these experiential modalities reflect certain conceptual commitments. It will become evident that the experience of real gratuitous evil rests on conceptual commitments which logically exclude the principle of meticulous providence.

One aspect of the experience of the tragic is that of the transience of value in human life. This does not mean that value itself passes, but that things of value, instances of value, last only for a time. Regardless of how strongly we cherish the goods of existence (e.g., friendship, beauty, creativity, and even life itself), there persists the disturbing apprehension that they are fragile and fleeting. Some goods are destroyed and replaced by unmistakable evils. The existential sense of the temporal impermanence of value in the world is accented by the recognition of the ultimate and universal character of value itself. Values in the abstract sense are not simply the expression of personal desires or goals, and are not merely the objects of social consensus. Values are transcendent and intensely precious; their claim upon our lives is absolute and nonnegotiable. It is in this light that the inevitable diminution of value in human experience may indeed be tragic.

The sheer transience of value in human existence, though a necessary condition for experience of the tragic, is not a sufficient one. Obviously, the transience of value per se is not always tragic. The value of initial cordiality must give way to the value of deeper friendship; the pianist must allow each note to die in turn in order that other beautiful notes may live. It is when there is unnecessary frustration or premature termination of value that the sense of the tragic properly arises. The very creation of value is often contingent upon situations which are themselves impermanent and subject to drastic change. This seems to put the actualization and continuation of value out of our complete control and make it subject to what is sometimes fortuitous and alien. So the tragic sense is constituted by the experience not merely of the passing of value, but of its senseless and gratuitous passing.

This is the tragic sense which gripped Doctor Rieux and caused him to reject the answers of Paneloux in *The Plague*. The stricken child deserved to live and be fulfilled, and yet its life was senselessly snuffed out; no conceptual contrivance could explain this away. But as long as Paneloux believed that all present evils contribute to greater goods, perhaps to goods known only to the divine wisdom, then he could not be struck by the deep sense of tragedy which the child's ordeal occasioned in Rieux.

Just as we must accept gratuitous evil on the conceptual level, we must not shut out the impact of gratuitous evil on the experiential level. If this suggestion is basically correct—that the sense of gratuitous evil is part of the complete range of legitimate human responses—it is *a fortiori* part of the range of Christian responses. But if conditioned by the principle of meticulous providence, or some version of it, the experience of evil may be doomed to triviality, never capturing the significance of man's precarious venture in the realm of values. It can be argued, therefore, that only by rejecting the conceptual commitment to meticulous providence can we fully experience the utterly pointless destruction of good and the devastating presence of evil in the world.

Dealing with the Experience of Gratuitous Evil

The experience of senseless, pointless evil demands a careful response. How can we deal with this experience and fit it into the whole of life? One response is given by Miguel de Unamuno in his modern masterpiece, *Tragic Sense of Life*. The Spanish philosopher explores the human longing for personal immortality. The book is permeated with the question of whether the pursuit of value— indeed, whether the living of life itself—is worth it, if life does not endure eternally. In his own inimical way, Unamuno writes:

> Must I again declare to you the supreme vacuity of culture, of science, of art, of good, of truth, of beauty, of justice . . . of all these beautiful conceptions, if at the last, in four days or in four millions of centuries—it matters

not which—no human consciousness shall exist to appropriate this civilization, this science, art, good, truth, beauty, justice, and all the rest?[10]

Unamuno takes the fleeting character of value as grounds for the belief that life is tragic. He suggests that anyone who does not possess this perception is emotionally shallow.

One need not share Unamuno's pessimistic perspective on the fleeting nature of life. Unamuno rightly rejects the superficial position that the tragic sense is based on the frustration of one's own private desires and preferences. The tragic sense has to do with something much more profound and disturbing than that: the really important sense of tragedy pertains to the unwanted and ill-timed diminution of the values of life. However, Unamuno exaggerates the conclusion which should be drawn from this fact. He concludes that life itself—all of life—is tragic if value cannot be permanent within it. While those who call life tragic because it thwarts their personal preferences are trapped in a hollow form of solipsism, Unamuno's "tragic sense," based merely on the temporal aspects of value, seems inordinately sentimental. Both extremes are wrong.

Life itself is not tragic, but it includes the tragic. The soul which properly experiences real life will not find it tragic per se, but will find tragic elements in it. The reason for saying that life as a whole is not tragic is quite straightforward. We can correctly repudiate the idea that the fragile and fleeting nature of value renders the attempt to create it pointless. The fact that attempts to realize values sometimes fail, and the fact that realized values are inevitably swept away by the inexorable flow

10. Miguel de Unamuno, *Tragic Sense of Life*, trans. J. Crawford Flitch (New York: Dover, 1954), p. 96.

of time, elicit despair only in those who do not fully comprehend what value and its attainment are all about. The intrinsic quality of value is not lost because its embodiment in human affairs does not last forever. The quest for and achievement of value within this perishing, temporal life are worthwhile for their own sake. The aesthetic pleasure one enjoys today may fade away tomorrow; the good deeds one performs in this life may be forgotten after his death. But the appearance of such values in human existence renders life intensely meaningful and important, and prevents it from being utterly tragic. Temporal life, then, has supreme value because eternal values are sought and found in it. The creation of value in temporal life has ultimate significance.

Whenever love, joy, freedom, dignity, and a host of other goods are instantiated, an absolute and eternal quality is introduced into human experience. The instances of these goods may pass away, but nothing—not even God—can make it to be that they never were. John Bennett captures this point with poetic genius in "On an Old Photograph of Young Men and Women at a Picnic":

> Six young men and women sit
> somewhere in the simple country
> at a meadow's edge where tree shade
> dapples bent grasses.
>
> Behind them
> a rail fence straggles uphill. The fence is odd,
> at least for Wisconsin. Overhead
> the thrusting splay of a pine branch
> mentions the sky.
>
> They pose
> deep in their innocent summer
> and make the usual gestures.
>
> One young man with sideburns

and a grenadier's leap of mustache
holds up his mug of beer,
its froth rising upward forever.
The girl sitting next to him,
her blond hair tamed in a strict coil,
rests her slim hand on his shoulder.
Aphrodite in shirtwaist and ruffles,
she, too, is forever
and knows nothing at all of Yeats.
The photographer, doubly anonymous,
has fulfilled his joyous commission
during this lapse of a moment.

Six young men and women sit
at the edge of eden-meadow
in dappled pine shade and sunlight.
Incredibly vibrant and handsome,
they are, I suppose, three courting couples.

Time is a one-way glass for any Now
that opens only always on the Past;
not knowing it, they look clear-eyed
into the camera lens toward sixty years
and cannot see me in this unformed day.
But I watch them within the photograph
and my heart moves back toward theirs
in their flaming changeless summer.
They are becoming what they have become;
pure actual occasions both doomed and immortal.

There past the faintly crazed surface,
purely there, and there nameless
in puffed sleeves and ribbons,
in stiff collars and striped shirts,
and there, too, in the depth of lost time
and the joy of their burning bodies,
they move from being to being,
forever and ever becoming
pure actual occasions,
pure human occasions.

I do not know their names.
Circa 1910. Before the War,
somewhere in Wisconsin.
No one remembers their names.

I only know that for a brief while
they existed in the real world,
that for a brief while
they laughed in warm sunlight
and loved one another forever,
posed on the bright edge of eden-meadow.[11]

This poem affirms the very thesis offered above, namely, that there is intrinsic and enduring worth to the temporal achievement of value. (The point stands regardless of whether one adopts the process metaphysic suggested by the language of "pure occasions.")

If what has been argued regarding the temporal attainment of value is essentially correct, then the experience of gratuitous evil is not to be met with despair, but hope. The same general conditions which make possible the tragic passing of value are the very conditions which also make possible its creation: freedom, creativity, and the neutrality of the external world. And the creation of positive value, though it may last only for a time, is worth it.

When we augment the human quest for value with a Christian perspective, it takes on even greater significance. Christianity holds that it is God who provides the conditions for the human creation of value and hence that man becomes a cocreator of value with Him. Thus there can be religious hope in the midst of senseless evil.

We should first determine what is entailed by the statement that the Christian theist can experience the creation of value as a partnership with God. Put negatively, the

11. John Bennett, *Griefs and Exultations* (West De Pere, WI: St. Norbert College, 1970), pp. 5–8.

statement does not entail that God is somehow limited by factors beyond His control and thus needs human co-operation to achieve His purposes.[12] Actually, the statement suggests only that for God to guarantee the success of good and prevent gratuitous evil would be for Him to jeopardize the significance of the human struggle for value. As argued in chapter 5, for God to preclude the possibility of gratuitous evils would also be for Him to preclude the possibility of some meaningful goods.

A second point is that the experience of being cocreator of value along with God includes a sense of the precariousness of man's position in a world of fragile and fleeting values. There are simply no divine guarantees that our struggles for good in this life will succeed. Although God ordains the quest for values, the ever-present possibility of cherished goods being tragically destroyed by human as well as nonhuman forces continually haunts us. Hence, there is no place for excessive religious optimism, such as that sometimes displayed by adherents to the principle of meticulous providence. And yet this possibility need not lead to a paralyzing pessimism, such as that shown by Camus's Doctor Rieux. Rieux believes that the world is hostile to human values, that it is an immoral world. Despite the negative aspects of existence, the Christian theist experiences the world as a context for the creation of value in which God plays a part—indeed, as a place in which God has already made decisive moves in the struggle for all that is good.

This brings us to a third point regarding the Christian experience of the creation of value. The life and work of Jesus Christ, when seen in the categories we have been using, is God's decisive blow in the struggle for good and

12. Edgar Brightman, e.g., understands deity as limited in specific ways and thus in need of human partnership. For a critique of all versions of finitism, see Keith Yandell, "The Problem of Evil," paper delivered at the Wheaton Annual Philosophy Conference, October 1980.

against evil. Our existential involvement in the struggle is enhanced by identification with the figure of Jesus Christ.[13] In a very real sense, the suffering and death of Jesus serve as a paradigm case of utterly senseless and horrible evil: a man who had done nothing but good was brutally tortured and killed. The Christian affirmation that this man is God incarnate entails that God Himself understands immediately and directly our pains and sufferings, and our feelings of helplessness and vulnerability in the face of the destructive forces of evil. The resurrection of Jesus Christ, then, is tragedy turned to triumph. Evil could not dominate. In the death and resurrection of Jesus Christ, the present potency of evil is diminished, the struggle for good empowered, and the final victory assured.

Reference to the kind of victory over evil which Jesus made possible is not inconsistent with the belief that some evil will remain forever gratuitous. In a certain sense of gratuitous evil—particularly a deontological sense—it is not clear *how* many horrible evils could ever be justified. And, according to the line of reasoning in this book, it is perhaps wrong-headed to expect such justification. The eschaton, then, need not be envisioned as a future state in which all evils are compensated for or made meaningful. Part of God's plan seems to be to place on man's shoulders the burden, at once ennobling and awesome, of creating or destroying values in a way which can never totally be revoked. God's culmination of all things and the manifestation of His kingdom must, therefore, include a kind of tragic beauty—a beauty wrought in spite of the fact that every evil cannot be requited. In no way does this imply that these evils are somehow justified because of some higher harmony or eternal bliss. It simply affirms

13. "Identification" here means, at a minimum, accepting His salvation and attempting to live according to His will. The term also suggests some degree of reflective understanding of the relation of Jesus Christ to good and evil in the world.

that God has chosen to take the human enterprise seriously, even if that means that irrevocable evil is sometimes produced. But it also affirms that He fully intends to accomplish His will and establish an everlasting kingdom in a way consonant with that enterprise.

The real triumph over evil should be understood as occurring now in the spirits of the redeemed and ultimately in the destruction of the structures of evil which dominate this age. This is the decisive conquest over evil which Jesus announced in the midst of history and which will be culminated at the end of history. Until that final time, we must continue to live in a world where genuine tragedy can occur, where evil sometimes seems invincible and good so transient. This is the grand risk of God's program; no other program can compare with the exquisite one which He has initiated on our behalf. The theist who understands this venture in values—the opportunities for realizing them and the chances of losing them—has attained an important glimpse into the meaning of life itself. The Christian theist can have confidence that God is with him in this venture, helping him resist evil and do good.[14] Although there are no guarantees that one will be successful in every endeavor in the realm of values, the Christian theist can know that God will use his efforts for eternal purposes.

The function of the christological motif here should not be misunderstood. It is not meant to imply that there is no ultimately gratuitous evil, and thus proffer a type of greater-good theodicy. Neither is it intended to offer experiential "absolution" from coming up with a theoret-

14. This in no way implies that God is just going along with our program. In a real sense, the human venture is His program. But it is His program for us. He cannot, therefore, always, or even frequently, intervene in direct ways. For the most part, He helps, guides, encourages, and empowers; the initiative within this context, then, is ours.

ical solution to the problem. Insofar as the problem of evil calls theism into question, it strikes at the foundations of Christianity. Therefore, Christianity cannot initially be employed to defend theism or to generate a theodicy. However, once theism is properly defended, it is perfectly legitimate to draw from the resources of Christian thought in order to develop a full theodicy.

The christological motif in the present discussion is designed to be a key to how the Christian theist may relate himself existentially to the world. When the principle of meticulous providence is relinquished and an alternative rendering of God's relation to evil is given, the way is open for the theistic believer to experience the world through different categories. The figure of Jesus Christ, though unique in certain important respects, goes a long way toward supplying these categories. Jesus Christ experienced fully the severe evil and tragedy in the world and responded with aggressive goodness. Upon recognizing the gratuitous evil in our world and the ever-present possibility of its increase, we too should strive against it and endeavor to produce good. The figure of Christ is God's proof that He feels the struggle with us and supplies strength to continue. Nowhere in the words and deeds of Christ is it suggested that the earthly search for value must automatically be successful or that our emotional response to evil should always be tranquil and optimistic. Instead the complete range of legitimate human emotions is found in the person of Christ. The christological motif envisioned here makes room for real failure and real tragedy, and it gives a place even to the emotions of anguish and rage. This motif also incorporates the idea that there is a kind of stern justice in the unalterable conditions of the human endeavor. But it also accents the fact that the presence of God in the struggle gives special hope.

The Existential Problem of Evil
and Christian Commitment

The existential awareness of gratuitous evil is only one aspect of our total lived experience. Hence, it is only one of numerous factors relevant to the final acceptance or rejection of Christian theism. Earlier in this chapter, we saw that the experience of tragic, pointless evil, considered in itself, does not disconfirm a conceptually adequate theistic system. In this section, we will examine how the experience of evil functions within the larger context of thought and life, and then try to determine its bearing on the viability of Christian theism.

We can begin to place the problem of evil in context by reviewing exactly how both its theoretical and existential formulations have been handled within the scope of this book. First, we have seen that the theoretical problem of gratuitous evil has force only if the principle of meticulous providence holds. As long as the principle is mistakenly attributed to Christian theism, the obvious facts of gratuitous evil will constitute a strong, and perhaps a sufficient, reason for the rejection of theism. The strategy for rebutting the theoretical problem of evil is straightforward. We should not deny or distort the gratuitous evils of common experience; rather we should rethink certain elements within the conceptual structure of theism and eventually reject the spurious principle of meticulous providence. Doing this not only rebuts the theoretical problem of evil, but also suggests a more realistic and profound understanding of Christian theism.

Second, we have seen that the existential objection from evil loses much of its force when the theoretical structure of Christian theism is properly understood. Since there is an intimate connection between concept and experience, it is quite natural that the significance attributed to one's experience changes when one's thinking changes. Hence, the tendency for the experience of gratuitous evil to lead toward an atheistic conclusion is greatly reduced when the principle of meticulous providence is removed from the conception of Christian theism. In fact, a stronger thesis might be urged to the effect that the proper conceptual change not only reduces the tendency toward atheism, but also gives the experience of gratuitous evil a measure of theistic significance. In other words, having the proper categories for the role of evil allows one to perceive a *theistic* world—albeit one in which meaningless evil is both possible and actual.

At this point, a symmetry has been developed between the theoretical and existential responses to gratuitous evil. In responding to the theoretical problem, we showed first that gratuitous evil does not disconfirm theism. Then we showed that, to the contrary, gratuitous evil can be so construed as to confirm theism. Now, in responding to the existential problem, we have likewise argued that the experience of gratuitous evil need not lead to the conclusion that we are perceiving a nontheistic world. Instead, we are perceiving a complex and profound theistic world, a perception mediated in part by gratuitous evil.

After showing that the theoretical and existential problems of evil can be effectively rebutted, much more remains to be said in appraising theism. The burden of this book is to argue that the problem of evil—even in its most severe form—can be refuted, and that it can even be turned into a subtle confirmation of Christian theism. There are many other considerations, both theoretical and existential, which are relevant. Moreover, there are other worldviews, both religious and secular, which compete with theism. These competing views, which must also be carefully evaluated, encounter their own distinct problems of evil.[15] All of this makes the issue of Christian theism quite complicated. What we are left with, then, is the grueling but rewarding task of sifting and weighing all of the arguments pertinent to Christian theism and its rivals. There is no simple formula for completing this evaluation, but there is no responsible way of avoiding it either. We must proceed with humility and tolerance, fairness and good sense. For many who have taken up the task, Christian theism is a conceptually and experientially adequate world-and-life view, more adequate than alternative views.

15. E.g., all major world religions are faced with explaining evil in terms of their own conceptual frameworks; also, a variety of secular philosophies, such as Marxism and naturalism, must do the same. An assumption of this book is that these competing systems do not handle their problems of evil as well as Christian theism handles its problem. Furthermore, it is assumed that the responses generated on the basis of Christian theism are more consonant with common human experience than are the responses of any alternative system.

Selected Bibliography

Books

Ahern, M. B. *The Problem of Evil.* New York: Schocken Books, 1971.

Bowker, John. *Problems of Suffering in Religions of the World.* New York: Cambridge University, 1970.

Ferré, Nels. *Evil and the Christian Faith.* New York: Harper and Brothers, 1947.

Galligan, Michael. *God and Evil.* New York: Paulist, 1976.

Geach, Peter T. *Providence and Evil.* New York: Cambridge University, 1977.

Griffin, David Ray. *God, Power, and Evil: A Process Theodicy.* Philadelphia: Westminster, 1976.

Hick, John. *Evil and the God of Love.* Revised edition. New York: Harper and Row, 1975.

Joad, C. E. M. *God and Evil.* New York: Harper and Brothers, 1943.

Journet, Charles. *The Meaning of Evil.* Translated by Michael Barry. New York: P. J. Kenedy and Sons, 1963.

Lewis, C. S. *The Problem of Pain.* New York: Macmillan, 1962.

Madden, Edward, and Hare, Peter. *Evil and the Concept of God.* Springfield, IL: Charles C. Thomas, 1968.

Maritain, Jacques. *God and the Permission of Evil.* Translated by Joseph Evans. Milwaukee: Bruce, 1966.

Plantinga, Alvin. *God, Freedom, and Evil.* Grand Rapids: Eerdmans, 1977.

————. *The Nature of Necessity.* New York: Oxford University, 1974.

Schilling, S. Paul. *God and Human Anguish.* Nashville: Abingdon, 1977.

Sontag, Frederick. *The God of Evil: An Argument from the Existence of the Devil.* New York: Harper and Row, 1970.

Articles

Aiken, Henry D. "God and Evil: A Study of Some Relations Between Faith and Morals." *Ethics* 68 (1958): 77–97.

Basinger, David. "Evil as Evidence Against the Existence of God: A Response." *Philosophy Research Archives,* 17 February 1978.

Dore, Clement. "Do Theists Need to Solve the Problem of Evil?" *Religious Studies* 12 (1976): 383–89.

————. "Ethical Supernaturalism and the Problem of Evil." *Religious Studies* 8 (1972): 97–113.

Flew, Antony. "Divine Omnipotence and Human Freedom." In *New Essays in Philosophical Theology,* edited by Antony Flew and Alasdair MacIntyre, pp. 144–69. New York: Macmillan, 1964.

Hoitenga, Dewey, Jr. "Logic and the Problem of Evil." *American Philosophical Quarterly* 4 (1967): 114–26.

Kane, G. Stanley. "The Failure of Soul-Making Theodicy." *International Journal for Philosophy of Religion* 6 (1975): 1–22.

————. "The Free-Will Defense Defended." *New Scholasticism* 50 (1976): 435–46.

Kohák, Erazim. "The Person in a Personal World: An Inquiry into the Metaphysical Significance of the Tragic Sense of Life." *Independent Journal of Philosophy* 1 (1977): 51–64.

LaCroix, Richard R. "Unjustified Evil and God's Choice." *Sophia* 13 (1974): 20–28.

Mackie, J. L. "Evil and Omnipotence." *Mind* 64 (1955): 200–12.

Martin, Michael. "Is Evil Evidence Against the Existence of God?" *Mind* 87 (1978): 429–32.

Pargetter, Robert. "Evil as Evidence Against the Existence of God." *Mind* 85 (1976): 242–45.

Peterson, Michael L. "Christian Theism and the Problem of Evil." *Journal of the Evangelical Theological Society* 21 (1978): 35–46.

――――. "Evil and Inconsistency." *Sophia* 18 (1979): 20–27.

――――. "God and Evil: Problems of Consistency and Gratuity." *Journal of Value Inquiry* 13 (1979): 305–13.

Pike, Nelson. "God and Evil: A Reconsideration." *Ethics* 68 (1958): 116–24.

――――. "Plantinga on the Free Will Defense: A Reply." *Journal of Philosophy* 63 (1966): 93–104.

Plantinga, Alvin. "Pike and Possible Persons." *Journal of Philosophy* 63 (1966): 104–08.

――――. "The Probabilistic Argument from Evil." *Philosophical Studies* 35 (1979): 1–53.

Reichenbach, Bruce. "Must God Create the Best Possible World?" *International Philosophical Quarterly* 19 (1979): 203–12.

――――. "Natural Evils and Natural Laws: A Theodicy for Natural Evils." *International Philosophical Quarterly* 16 (1976): 179–96.

Salmon, Wesley. "Religion and Science: A New Look at Hume's *Dialogues*." *Philosophical Studies* 33 (1978): 143–76.

Smart, Ninian. "Omnipotence, Evil and Supermen." *Philosophy* 36 (1961): 188–95.

Yandell, Keith. "A Premature Farewell to Theism (A Reply to Roland Pucetti)." *Religious Studies* 5 (1969): 251–55.

Index